CONTENTS

KU-209-036

CHAPTER 1

Spain –
An Overview

Spain is a large, mountainous country occupying about 85 per cent of the Iberian Peninsula, which it shares with Portugal. In the north-east, the Pyrenean Mountains straddle Spain's 720-km (447-mile) border with France. Historically these mountains, with their relatively few passes, have isolated Spain and Portugal from the rest of Europe. Today, however, road and air links have enabled Spain to become fully integrated into the political and economic life of Europe, and it is now an important member of the European Union (EU). Besides its commercial and political links, Spain is one of Europe's most popular tourist destinations, attracting millions of European visitors each year, as well as others from all over the world.

Spain's capital is Madrid, a city situated in the centre of the country. Besides Madrid and Zaragoza (in the north-east), Spain's main population centres are in coastal regions, reflecting its history as a maritime (seafaring) nation. Some smaller inland settlements are important, however, because they are the capitals of Spain's 'autonomous regions' (see page 22). There are seventeen autonomous regions in all, thirteen on the mainland and four others, including the Balearic Islands (in the Mediterranean Sea), the Canary Islands (in the Atlantic Ocean), and the two enclaves of Ceuta and Melilla on Morocco's Mediterranean coast.

Spain is a diverse country with a wide range of climates, landscapes, people and cultures. It even has several distinct languages. Spanish (more correctly called Castilian, after its early origins in Cantabria and Castile) is the main language, but there are three other official languages: Basque,

? Did you know?

Castilian, Catalan and Galician are derived from Latin and, along with French and Italian, are known as the Romance languages. However, the Basque regional language, known as Euskera, is completely unique. It has neither vocabulary nor grammar in common with any other known language.

◄ Spaniards use markets for socializing as well as buying the very best local produce.

Catalan and Galician, each of which relates to a specific region of Spain. Spain's autonomous regions can be described as several countries contained within the state of Spain, in the same way that England, Scotland, Wales and Northern Ireland make up the UK.

REGIONAL DIFFERENCES

The Basque Country lies at the northern end of the Pyrenees, a mountain chain on either side of the French-Spanish border. It is an important industrial region, with heavy industries such as steelworks and shipbuilding. With its temperate climate, green fields and dense woodland, the Basque Country feels and looks very different from the picture postcard images of 'sunny Spain' and its coastal resorts.

▼ For all its variety, Spain's towns and cities have much in common, including shady streets with café terraces and lots of people.

Galicia is a wild, rugged region in north-west Spain, bordering the Atlantic Ocean to the north and west and Portugal to the south. The original inhabitants of Galicia were of Celtic origin and the region shares many cultural aspects with Ireland and Scotland, such as the playing of bagpipes and sword-dancing. Fishing is economically important here, though the conditions along its treacherous coastline are summed up by the name, *La Costa de la Muerte*, 'The Coast of Death'!

Catalonia, in eastern Spain, is marked by the influence of its former Roman conquerors. Here the Romans founded many trading centres that were later to become great cities, such as the Catalan capital, Barcelona. The Romans traded local produce, including wheat, olives, vines (plants producing grapes used to make wine) and vegetables. These cities remain important commercial and industrial centres today.

In southern Spain, the Andalucía region has an arid landscape which occasionally gives way to oases of deep-green foliage and cultivated river valleys. Arabic peoples (known as Moors) from North Africa occupied southern Spain for seven centuries (between 711 and 1492) and their influence is visible in the local architecture – from grand, historic buildings to simple homes. The Moors introduced sophisticated irrigation systems to the deltas and inland seas on Spain's Mediterranean and Atlantic coasts.

Physical geography

- Land area: 499,542 sq km/192,873 sq miles
- Water area: 5,240 sq km/2,023 sq miles
- Total area: 504,782 sq km/194,896 sq miles
- World rank (by area): 51
- Land boundaries: 1,918 km/1,191 miles
- Border countries: Andorra, France, UK (at Gibraltar), Portugal, Morocco
- Coastline: 4,964 km/3,083 miles
- Highest point: Pico de Teide (Tenerife) (3,718m/12,198 ft)
- Lowest point: Atlantic Ocean (0 m/0 ft)

Source: CIA World Factbook

THE SPANISH INTERIOR

The interior of Spain consists of a large plateau called the *Meseta Central*. The *Meseta* covers an area of some 210,000 sq km (81,000 sq miles) and has an average elevation of 700 m (2,300 ft). The city of Madrid lies at the centre of the *Meseta* and has been the Spanish capital since 1607. It was chosen by King Phillip II as a centralized location from which to unify Spain's smaller states into a single kingdom, and has maintained a dominant role ever since, whether in the arts, industry, politics or commerce.

A FRAGILE UNION?

Some of Spain's regions, especially the Basque Country and Catalonia, have frequently vied for greater autonomy or complete independence from the central government. This has given Spain a history of internal conflict that continues to this day, for example, with the terrorist actions of the Basque separatist group, ETA. Despite these pressures, Spain remains a united, politically stable and highly developed country with an economy that is one of the most prosperous and fastest growing in the EU.

◀ The Basque Country is famous for its cuisine, which is heavily dependent on fish harvested from around its coastline.

Map labels

Bay of Biscay

FRANCE

A Coruña
Gijón
Santander
Santiago de Compostela
Oviedo
ASTURIAS
PICOS DE EUROPA
CANTABRIA
Bilbao
Guernica
San Sebastián-Donostia
GALICIA
CORDILLERA CANTÁBRICA
BASQUE COUNTRY
PYRENEES
ANDORRA
Vigo
Ourense
León
Vitoria-Gastiez
Pamplona
Aneto 3404m
0°
2°
42°
Burgos
Logroño
NAVARRA
Huesco
Girona
Costa Brava
42°
CASTILLE-LEÓN
LA RIOJA
Ebro
Zaragoza
CATALONIA
Duero
Valladolid
Lleida
8°
Zamora
ARAGÓN
Barcelona
SPAIN
Salamanca
Tarragona
Segovia
Guadalajara
SIERRA DE GUADARRAMA
★ **MADRID**
Teruel
Balearic Islands
4°
Menorca
40°
MADRID
Castelló
Mahon
Tagus
Palma de Mallorca
4°
Toledo
Valencia
Mallorca
PORTUGAL
EXTREMADURA
CASTILLE-LA MANCHA
VALENCIA
Ibiza
Merida
Albacete
2°
Badajoz
Alcoy
SIERRA MORENA
Elche
Alicante
Mediterranean Sea
38°
Córdoba
Murcia
Costa Blanca
38°
Jaén
MURCIA
Guadalquivir
ANDALUCIA
Cartagena
0°
Huelva
Seville
Granada
Mulhacén 3404m
SIERRA NEVADA
Almería
Jerez
Cádiz
Málaga
Costa del Sol
Marbella
Algeciras
Gibraltar
36°
Ceuta
36°
Straits of Gibraltar
ATLANTIC OCEAN
Melilla
ALGERIA
6°
4°
2°
MOROCCO

Islas Canarias (Canary Islands)

18°
14°
La Palma
Lanzarote
Santa Cruz de la Palma
16°
Fuerteventura
Santa Cruz de Tenerife
Pico de Teide 3718m
Las Palmas
28°
La Gomera
Tenerife
28°
Gran Canaria
Hierro
18°
16°
14°

Legend

★ Capital
● Cities > 1,000,000
● Cities > 500,000
• Cities > 200,000
· other cities
▲ Mountain

0   50   100 kilometres
0   50   100 miles
N

History

Early evidence of prehistoric settlement in Spain dates back 280,000 years. The country's documented history begins with the Phoenicians who, attracted by Spain's mineral wealth, had arrived in the south by 800 BC. From around 575 BC the Greeks developed trading interests in Spain, but their settlement was limited to the eastern coast. The Phoenicians and Greeks influenced indigenous populations and gave rise to a distinctive Iberian culture from around 550 BC.

ROMAN SPAIN

In 218 BC, Roman troops arrived in Spain to disrupt Phoenician supply routes between Spain and Carthage, the Phoenician capital in Tunisia (Rome was engaged in a power struggle with the Phoenicians). During the next two centuries, and following numerous wars with various tribes, the Romans colonized the Iberian Peninsula. They called their colonized lands 'Hispania'. They divided the lands into provinces, gave settlements a Roman form, and built bridges, aqueducts and roads. In AD 410, however, Rome was attacked by barbarians from northern and eastern Europe, including a Germanic people known as Visigoths. The Visigoths went on to invade Spain, where they integrated with the Roman settlers and adopted Christianity. By AD 584, the Visigoth King Leogivild had established a kingdom covering the whole peninsula, with Toledo as its capital.

ISLAM AND CHRISTIANITY

Feuding among the Visigoth nobility and political disorganization throughout the country weakened Spain and left it open to an Arab invasion from North Africa. In 711 the Arabs, or Moors, defeated the Visigoths in battle and within three years had conquered most of the peninsula. The arrival of Islam brought a new energy to southern Spain and prompted a flowering of art, literature, architecture and scholarship. Isolated Christian communities retreated to the north-west where

◀ The Roman aqueduct at Tarragona: Roman engineering supplied domestic water to important cities and for agriculture.

they began to plan the *reconquista* (reconquest) of Spain as a Christian state. Between the eleventh and the thirteenth centuries, the grip of the Islamic rulers gradually weakened. They were defeated at Toledo in 1085, at Valencia in 1094 and, in 1212, by a united Christian Spanish and Portuguese army at the Battle of Las Navas de Tolosa. The increasingly powerful Christian armies pushed further south, and soon only Granada remained under Moorish control. The new Christian Spain was dominated by the powerful states of Aragón and Castile.

THE CATHOLIC KINGS

In 1469 Ferdinand, heir to the throne of Aragón, married Isabella of Castile and began the unification of Spain's Catholic kingdoms. This process was completed when Ferdinand came to the throne in 1479. In 1492, King Ferdinand II and Queen Isabella forced the Muslims to surrender their last stronghold of Granada to Spain. In the same year, the 'Catholic Kings' used their powers to expand Spanish ambitions abroad, sponsoring Christopher Columbus's voyages of discovery to the New World of the Americas. Their influence also saw a Spaniard, Alexander VI, take up the office of pope in Rome, a position he used in 1494 to grant Spain rights to explore the New World. In their pursuit of a powerful Catholic kingdom, Ferdinand and Isabella established the Spanish

Inquisition to root out what they saw as the evil of other religious doctrines. Muslims, Jews and people of other faiths were forced to convert to Catholicism and persecuted or expelled if they failed to do so. In 1492, some 170,000 Jews who refused to be baptized into Catholicism were expelled from Spain.

▼ Detail of a tapestry recording the meeting of King Ferdinand and Queen Isabella with Christopher Columbus in the Saló de Tinell in Barcelona.

THE RISE AND FALL OF AN EMPIRE

Ferdinand died in 1516 and the Spanish throne passed to his grandson, Charles I, ruler of the Netherlands and heir to the Habsburg kingdom of Austria and southern Germany. Charles succeeded to the Habsburg throne in 1519 and in doing so made Spain part of the most powerful empire of the time. There followed a 'golden age', with Spanish explorers venturing further into the Americas, conquering Mexico (in 1519), Peru (in 1532) and Chile (in 1541). The explorers amassed great riches for Spain, but also destroyed entire indigenous civilizations. Charles used the gold and silver they seized to fund wars against the growth of Protestantism and in defence of the Catholic faith.

The early seventeenth century saw remarkable artistic and architectural achievements in Spain with, for example, the paintings of Velázquez and El Greco, the writings of Cervantes and the construction of the spectacular Plaza Mayor in Madrid. But Spain's political and economic power was increasingly threatened by other European nations, such as the Netherlands, England and France. In 1700, the death of the childless Charles II brought the Habsburg line to an end. The Spanish throne passed to Phillip V, grandson of the French King Louis XIV and member of the great Bourbon dynasty.

WARS OF SUCCESSION

Between 1702 and 1714 a power struggle known as the War of the Spanish Succession took place in Europe. The French supported the Bourbon king, Phillip V, while the British, Dutch and Austrians, disliking this extension of French influence, supported the Austrian Archduke Charles. The Bourbons won the day, however, and began to centralize power in Spain. But over the next hundred years there followed further wars of succession involving

▼ The Plaza Mayor in Madrid, built around 1620.

foreign powers. In the Peninsular War (also known as the War of Independence), French troops under Napoleon Bonaparte occupied the whole of Spain but were defeated in 1809 by a combination of Spanish resistance fighters and British forces under the Duke of Wellington.

In the nineteenth century, Spain lost large parts of its empire to other European powers. Its American colonies, including Peru, Bolivia and Chile, were also in revolt and most of them achieved independence by the 1820s. Spain entered a period of political turmoil, with three more wars of succession (the Carlist Wars) and several *coups d'etat*, in which monarchists and republicans vied for control of the state. In 1868 the army, under General Prim, seized control in a revolution that attempted to establish a constitutional monarchy. This failed, however, and led to the declaration of Spain's First Republic in 1873. But the republic was disorganized and divided and, in December 1874, forces loyal to the monarchy restored a Bourbon king, Alfonso XII, to the Spanish throne.

INTO THE TWENTIETH CENTURY

The restoration of the monarchy brought about a period of industrialization and relative prosperity. Iron ore, wine and wool were among the main products, and all were in high demand in Europe. By the end of the nineteenth century, however, the boom was over and Spain was facing political challenges from its remaining colonies in Cuba, Puerto

▲ A nineteenth-century French illustration showing Napoleon Bonaparte's entry into Madrid.

Rico and the Philippines. In 1898, Spain suffered a damaging defeat in the Spanish-American War in which the remaining colonies gained their independence.

This downturn in Spanish fortunes led to widespread criticism of the restored monarchy and opposition to the existing political system. Domestic strikes and violence led to yet more discontent until, in 1923, General Miguel Primo de Rivera displaced the government and took control as dictator of Spain. He set about political and economic reforms, but his regime was generally unpopular and unstable.

 Did you know?

During the nineteenth century, Spain experienced five wars, eight overthrows of government, seven monarchies and six constitutions.

In 1930, King Alfonso XIII forced Primo de Rivera to resign. However, in 1931 Republican election victories and continued disquiet made it clear that the monarchy could not survive, and Alfonso was forced to abdicate. Spain's Second Republic was proclaimed, and a new government launched sweeping changes that included greater powers for the regions and extensive land reforms.

The aristocracy, landowners and monarchists began plotting a rebellion with military leaders, among them an army general named Francisco Franco. Known as 'Nationalists', the rebels allied themselves to Falange Española, a new political party that had emerged in 1933 under the leadership of Primo de Rivera's son, Antonio. The emergence of the fascist-inclined Falange was partly in response to the growth of socialism in Spanish politics and its association with communism. Spain became divided between socialists, communists, anarchists on the one hand and monarchists and fascists on the other. This division set the scene for the Spanish Civil War.

CIVIL WAR

The Spanish Civil War (1936-39) broke out in July 1936, when the Nationalists, under General Franco, orchestrated uprisings across Spain against the socialist Republican government. Army units loyal to the government together with heavily armed national police, the Guardia Civil, and workers' militias, undermined the rebel forces in the regions, but Franco responded by moving his troops and laying siege to Madrid. Volunteers from over fifty countries joined an International Brigade to fight for the Spanish Republic against what was perceived to be a rising tide of fascism. The Nationalists secured military support from fascist leaders Adolf Hitler in Germany and Benito Mussolini in Italy.

Facing tough resistance in Madrid, Franco moved the war to the north, capturing Spain's industrial districts. Catalonia and the Basque Country remained loyal to the Republican government because it had guaranteed them greater regional autonomy. On behalf of the Nationalists, German Nazi aircraft bombed the Basque town of Guernica in April 1937, subjecting ordinary civilians to the terrors of modern warfare for the first time. Nationalist forces slowly gained ground and divided the Republicans by capturing Valencia. The Republican army was devastated during the Battle of the Ebro in 1938, and the war finally ended when Madrid fell to the Nationalists in March 1939.

◀ Adolf Hitler (left) meets General Franco (right) for a conference near the French-Spanish border in 1940.

FRANCO'S SPAIN

In 1936 the Nationalists had granted Franco emergency powers as the head of state and government. At the end of the war, Franco took up these positions and governed Spain as a dictator, manipulating the Church, army and landowners to achieve his ends. During the Second World War (1939-45), Franco's sympathies were with Germany and Italy, but Spain remained neutral because it depended on the Allies for food and oil. After the war, Spain became isolated as the last fascist regime in Europe and was refused entry to the newly formed United Nations (UN). In 1955, as Franco's regime appeared to become less harsh and gain respectability, UN membership was eventually granted. But in reality Franco continued to rule through often brutal measures and his dictatorship lasted until his death in 1975.

▼ King Juan Carlos (third from right) and other members of the Spanish royal family watch a military parade outside Parliament in Madrid.

AFTER FRANCO

In 1969, Franco had nominated Alphonso XIII's grandson, Prince Juan Carlos de Bourbon, to succeed him, believing that a monarch would continue the fascist regime. But when Juan Carlos became king in 1975 he announced plans for a liberalized government and a new constitution guaranteeing human rights, social reforms, the separation of Church and State, and greater autonomy for the regions. The constitution was passed in 1978 and has been the basis of peaceful political transition in Spain ever since. The return of political stability saw the beginning of an economic recovery that continues today and paved the way for Spain to join the European Economic Union (EEC) in 1986.

 Did you know?

Guernica, one of Spanish artist Pablo Picasso's most famous works, was painted in protest at the bombing of the Basque capital during the Civil War.

CHAPTER 3

Landscape and Climate

The Spanish landscape is dominated by coasts and mountains. To the north and south-west of the country is the Atlantic Ocean; to the east and the south is the Mediterranean Sea. Large mountain ranges follow these coasts: the Cordillera Cantábrica and Picos de Europa on the north Atlantic seaboard, and the Sierra Nevada in Andalucía. The Littoral and Beatic mountain ranges extend under the Mediterranean Sea to form the Balearic Islands (Mallorca, Menorca, Cabrera, Ibiza and Formentera). In the north-east, the Pyrenees follow the border with France. The tallest mountain in the Pyrenees is Aneto at 3,404 m (11,168 ft).

Did you know?

The highest mountain in Spain is not on the mainland. It is the 3,718-m (12,198-ft) Pico de Tiede on the Canary Island of Tenerife.

The *Meseta Central* is a high, arid plateau that dominates Spain's interior and includes the regions of Aragón, Castile-Leon, Castile-La Mancha, Extremadura, Navarra and La Rioja. Two mountain ranges, the Sierra de Guadarrama and Sierra Morena, cross the *Meseta* from west to east. It is from these that many of Spain's important rivers originate.

VARIED COASTLINES

The Atlantic coastline of Galicia in north-western Spain is characterized by rugged cliffs and indented by fjords called *rias*. Further east, the coast becomes less dramatic and features sandy coves that are suitable for bathing. In the Basque Country, wide sandy beaches separate

▼ Life is hard in the remote *Meseta* villages. Much of the terrain is unsuitable even for wheat farming because the land is so uneven.

 In the Ebro delta, lush vegetation and rice paddies thrive in the combination of warm Mediterranean climate and river water from the wet north coast of Spain.

green fields from the sea. The southern Atlantic coastline is mainly flat and includes the important Doñana coastal wetlands in the delta of the Guadalquivir River. These are a vital habitat for migratory birds travelling between Europe and Africa, and around half of all European bird species can be found there.

The Mediterranean coast extends from the Straits of Gibraltar in the south to the French border at Cap Creus. This coastline is characterized by narrow, fertile plains backed by steep mountains that, in places, sweep down to the sea. Numerous rivers have cut deep ravines through these mountains, and deltas have formed where the larger ones meet the sea. The wetlands of the Ebro River delta are particularly significant for wildlife and agriculture.

HUMAN EFFECTS ON THE LANDSCAPE

The Mediterranean regions of Spain are the most densely populated and economically important in the country. The impact of people on the landscape is clear, not least in the so-called 'concrete wall' of hotels and seaside

resorts that caters for Spain's huge tourist industry. The landscape has also been shaped by more than 2,000 years of agriculture. Coastal plains, deltas, and two large lagoons – La Albufera in Valencia and Mar Menor in Murcia – have been drained and irrigated to produce fertile farmland. In the mountains, terraces have been cut into the land to provide level ground for the cultivation of tree crops such as olives, almonds, hazelnuts and citrus fruits.

 Did you know?

Spain's longest river, the Ebro, meanders south-eastwards for 910 km (565 miles) from the Picos de Europa to Catalonia, where it discharges into the Mediterranean.

 Did you know?

At 2,000 metres (6,562 ft), La Caldera de Taburiente on La Palma in the Canary Islands is the world's deepest volcanic crater and home to four unique plant species: *Viola palmensis*, *Echium gentianoides*, *Pterocephalus porphyranthus*, and *Tolpis calderae*.

ADAPTING TO CLIMATES

Most of Spain has a continental climate, with freezing winters and very hot summers. Spain's coastal mountains block the maritime winds and cause most of the rain to fall before it reaches the interior. This 'rainshadow effect' means that the *Meseta* is especially dry, with regular and severe droughts. Much of the *Meseta* is a stony, dry, windswept type of landscape known as badlands. Unsuitable for growing crops other than cereals, the *Meseta* is instead used for herding sheep and goats. Some shepherds still cover large distances with their herds, following routes that have been used since medieval times. The rocky mountainsides of the central *sierras* are covered in hardy variants of northern tree species such as pines, cork and scrub oaks, together with the *Alzina*, a native evergreen holm oak.

In the summer, daytime temperatures in Spain can soar to over 35°C (95°F). Before machinery transformed farming methods, people worked in the fields around dawn and dusk and spent the hottest part of the day eating and resting indoors – a period known as the *siesta*. Modern farm machinery has reduced the number of agricultural workers and the need to escape the heat of the day, but the *siesta* is still observed, and by more than just farming communities. Many offices, shops and factories close down between the hours of 1pm and 5pm, and reopen for the late afternoon and evening. Spaniards tend to socialize, shop and eat out in the evening when temperatures can fall by 15°C (27°F) or more.

CLIMATE TYPES

The Gulf Stream (a warm oceanic current that flows towards Europe from the Gulf of Mexico) has a major influence on Spain's north Atlantic coast. Its warm waters keep the climate here milder and wetter than it would otherwise be, with sufficient rainfall (annual average of around 1,400mm in Galicia) to support deciduous tree species not found elsewhere in

▼ Snow covers the alpine meadows of the Aiguestortes i Lac Sant Maurici national park in the Pyrenees.

Spain. In contrast, the coastal regions around the Gulf of Cádiz have a hot, arid climate in which annual rainfall can be less than 500mm (20 inches). The province of Huelva, west of Seville, has such high summer temperatures (over 40°C/104°F) that it is known as 'Spain's Oven'. Eastern coastal regions have a Mediterranean climate of hot, dry summers and warm winters. There are occasional climatic extremes, however, such as cloudbursts, known locally as *Gota Fria*, that can cause severe flash floods. Strong winds are another feature: the hot and humid 'Sirocco' wind often carries sands with it as it blows in from the Sahara Desert. Another wind, the cold, northerly 'Tramontana' howls around the eastern tip of the Pyrenees during the spring and autumn, buffeting Catalonia's northern coast – the Costa Brava or 'Fierce Coast'.

▲ Sea fjords, called *rias*, offer shelter for settlements along the stormy northern Atlantic coasts of Galicia and Asturias.

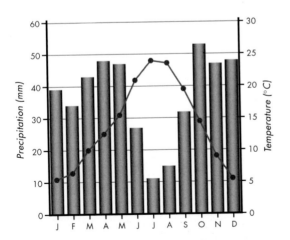

▲ Average monthly climate conditions in Madrid

 Did you know?

On average the southern Spanish cities of Granada and Seville receive 3,030 and 2,855 hours of sunshine respectively, but Santiago de Compostela in the north receives only 1,700 hours of sunshine.

Focus on: The Canary Islands

The seven volcanic islands of the Canary archipelago lie 100 km (60 miles) off the west coast of Morocco and cover 7,273 sq km (2,808 sq miles). They have varied landscapes: La Gomera supports lush subtropical vegetation on its fog-clad peaks, Lanzarote and Fuerteventura consist mainly of barren, volcanic debris and sand dunes. The isolation of the Canary Islands, combined with moist Atlantic winds and numerous microclimates, has enabled ancient plant species to survive the impact of the last ice ages. The Canaries are home to some 2,000 plant species. Many of these are unique to the islands and are protected within four of Spain's thirteen national parks. The warm climate of the Canary Islands makes them a popular holiday destination for northern Europeans from countries such as the UK and Germany.

CHAPTER 4

Population and Settlements

Spain's population of 40.5 million in 2008 is relatively small given the size of the country. Although Spain occupies more than twice the area of the UK, it has just two-thirds the number of people. Spain's coastal regions are the most densely populated parts of the country, while the centre is relatively unpopulated.

INTERNAL MIGRATION

The process of internal migration from Spain's countryside to its towns and cities began in earnest at the beginning of the nineteenth century. Ecological pressures, such as water shortages and crop diseases, together with the early mechanization of farming led to a reduced need for rural labour. Further mechanization of farming in the early twentieth century accelerated the decline in labour requirements and the associated depopulation of rural areas.

As Spain industrialized, new employment opportunities began to emerge in urban areas. In the Basque Country, nineteenth-century steel foundries and shipyards attracted large numbers of migrant labourers from other regions (particularly poorer southern regions like Andalucía and Extremadura). In parts of the Basque Country today, around half of the population is descended from these economic migrants. From around 1900, Catalonia also experienced considerable inward migration from other parts of Spain to provide labour for its growing textile industry. During the first half of the twentieth century, the Spanish Civil War and the Second World War had the effect of slowing down internal migration; but since the 1960s, when the Spanish economy began its recovery, rural to urban migration has increased.

EXTERNAL MIGRATION

During Franco's rule, around half a million Spaniards fled to France as refugees. Many of Spain's skilled workers also moved to West Germany during the 1950s and 1960s in search of better economic prospects. Since 1997, Spain has become a recipient of external migrants, most of whom arrive in search of employment. Economic migrants answer Spain's need for unskilled (and often temporary) labour, mainly in the agricultural and tourism sectors. Spain is a major horticultural (fruit, vegetables, herbs, flowers etc.) producer and requires significant

◀ Most Spanish cities have public areas where people can relax, as here, in the Plaça Reial, Barcelona.

numbers of workers at harvest times to carry out the unskilled jobs that many Spaniards are reluctant to do. The same is true for unskilled jobs in the tourist industry, including those of cleaners, porters and waiters.

Spain has an ageing population, which means the number of people working and paying tax has fallen, and the number of people drawing a pension and no longer working has risen. A solution would be to allow greater immigration to boost the working population. The majority of working age immigrants currently come from Spanish-speaking Latin America (38.6 per cent), or from African (and, especially, North African) countries (19.6 per cent).

Some migrants come to Spain out of choice rather than economic necessity. Its pleasant climate

Did you know?

Since 1986, the money transfer company Western Union has increased its agencies in Spain from twelve to over 5,000 to meet the needs of immigrants sending money home.

▲ New immigrants to Spain have difficulty finding work to fit their qualifications. This Nigerian chemist works as a labourer in a stone yard to support his young family.

Focus on: Illegal immigration

Illegal immigrants present Spain with a considerable challenge. On the one hand, Spain needs migrants to fill employment gaps, but on the other it must take responsibility for preventing illegal immigrants entering Spain or using it as a 'land bridge' into Europe. Many of Spain's illegal immigrants are smuggled from North Africa across the sea in small boats called *pateras*. They often suffer terrible conditions in their attempts to reach Spain and many even die on the journey. There is considerable public sympathy for immigrants trying to make a better life for themselves, as many Spaniards have also been migrants at some time. This sympathy is reflected in government policy: although borders are well controlled, once inside Spain, many illegal immigrants are helped to become legal residents. In 2005, during a three-month amnesty on illegal immigrants, the Spanish government formally accepted more than 700,000 illegal workers, allowing them and their dependents to live and work legally in Spain.

attracts many retired people from northern Europe, for example. As fellow EU members they are entitled to the same health and welfare support as Spaniards. This places the Spanish system under increasing pressure to provide for the elderly of other nations, as well as for its own ageing population. At 79.9 years, Spain has the second-highest life expectancy in Europe. The proportion of people over the age of 65 increased from 8 per cent in 1960 to 17 per cent by 2006, and is expected to reach almost 24 per cent by 2030.

CITIES AND THE *BARRIOS*

Many of Spain's cities retain their historic centres and have changed little in hundreds of years. In the seventeenth century, Spain's cities began to expand with the creation of new districts, called *barrios*, adjacent to the old centres. As people settled in the *barrios*, older urban areas were neglected and became squalid and unhealthy with only the poorest of people, often newly arrived migrants or immigrants, living there. As cities continued to expand, some of the older *barrios* also suffered in this way.

Since the 1980s, Spain has rejuvenated many of its run-down city centres and these have become popular with wealthy young Spaniards attracted by the plentiful supply of apartments and the social and cultural opportunities offered by city life. Historic buildings have been renovated and the streets are buzzing with life once again. In a reversal of past trends, the redevelopment of city centres is pushing poorer residents out into the surrounding *barrios* such as Lavapies in Madrid, or the Raval district in Barcelona. Despite the poverty, however, such districts are often vibrant, multicultural areas attracting a diverse population of immigrants and students because of their lower accommodation costs.

URBAN SPRAWL

During the last mass migrations to Spanish cities in the 1960s, large residential estates were built close to the new industrial zones where the majority of migrants worked. The estates were hurriedly built and poorly planned, with substandard buildings and a shortage of services (shops, leisure facilities, etc.). The estates also acted as a barrier to integration, as they tended to house mainly new migrants and were built away from city centres.

New estates are still being built on the outskirts of Spanish cities but, more often than not, these are now of the luxury variety known as *urbanizaciones*. These normally comprise terraced houses built around communal facilities like gardens and swimming pools. Their location on the city outskirts means that residents are heavily dependent on cars for

◄ *Barrios*, like El Raval in Barcelona have a bustling and noisy street life, but they provide a great sense of community.

getting to work, school or the shops. Cars are also vital for people who want to visit the large out-of-town shopping and entertainment complexes that have sprung up around the edge of most urban centres since the 1980s. Despite all this, most Spaniards still prefer to live in apartments in the city centre where everything is in close proximity. The Spaniards' love of a busy outdoor social life means that Spanish cities are lively and sociable places.

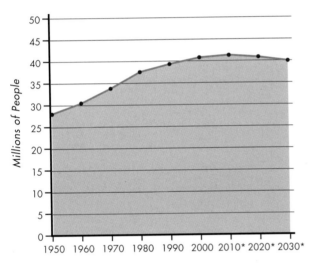

Projected Population

▲ Population growth 1950-2030

▲ Although many Spaniards would rather live in a house than a flat, the high cost of building land means that detached houses are rare.

Did you know?

At over 85.4 per cent, Spain has the highest home ownership rate in Europe. Between 1994 and 2004, second home ownership increased by 26 per cent to 2,628,817 dwellings.

Did you know?

Many young Spanish couples would rather save up to buy their first home than rent. This means that over 70 per cent of Spaniards under 29 years of age still live with their parents.

Population data

📁 Population: 40.5 million

📁 Population 0-14 yrs: 14%

📁 Population 15-64 yrs: 69%

📁 Population 65+ yrs: 17%

📁 Population growth rate: 0.1%

📁 Population density: 81.1 per sq km/ 210.0 per sq mile

📁 Urban population: 77%

📁 Major cities: Madrid 5,567,000
                  Barcelona 4,920,900

Source: United Nations, CIA and World Bank

CHAPTER 5

Government and Politics

Spain is a constitutional monarchy with a king as the head of state. The parliament, or *Cortes*, is based in Madrid and is the main political body in Spain. The seventeen autonomous regions also have their own parliaments and control areas such as healthcare, social services and public education. Several of the autonomous regions have their own laws, tax systems and even their own police forces. Of the seventeen regions, the Basque Country, Catalonia and Galicia have the greatest degree of control over their own affairs. Provincial governments, city and town councils (*ajuntamientos*) are responsible for various functions, such as urban planning control, local police and municipal services such as waste collection.

POLITICAL PARTIES

Support for the main political parties in Spain can be broadly divided by geography. In Madrid and southern Spain, the *Partido Socialista Obrero Español* (PSOE), or Spanish Socialist Workers' Party, is the controlling party. In most of northern Spain and in the smaller cities elsewhere, the *Partido Popular* (PP), or Spanish Conservative Party, is the dominant party. In Catalonia and the Basque Country, politics is complicated by a greater degree of autonomy and ambitions for independence from Spain. In Catalonia, for example, there are local political

▼ Spain's prime minister, José Luis Rodriguez Zapatero, delivers a speech in the *Cortes* in 2004.

parties, such as the Catalan Socialist Party (PSC) in addition to national parties like the PSOE and PP. The economic significance of Catalonia in Spain means that the Catalan parties are especially powerful. Since 1978, all Spanish governments have had to form coalitions with the Catalan parties at one time or another. These coalitions have given Catalonia considerable influence over national legislation as well as local issues, and some Spaniards feel that Catalonia has too much power. However, many Catalans (including those originating from other regions of Spain) feel that such powers are justified because the Catalan economy is disproportionately stronger and supports many poorer regions of Spain.

THE ESTABLISHMENT OF DEMOCRACY

Between 1939 and 1975, General Franco governed Spain as a brutal dictatorship. His successor, King Juan Carlos, initiated a new constitution in 1978 and laid the groundwork for Spain's present democratic system. The socialist PSOE came to power in 1979 under Felipe Gonzalez. After years of isolationist policies under Franco, the PSOE had the difficult task of rebuilding Spain as an integrated European nation. During the 1996 elections, accusations of corruption in the Gonzalez government resulted in it losing the support of the Catalan socialists. Consequently, the conservative PP came to power for the first time under José Maria Aznar. The Aznar government strengthened Spain's economic development, but failed, as had the Gonzalez government, to make significant progress over one of Spain's most important political issues, the future of the Basque Country.

 Did you know?

In Catalonia, 49 per cent of people speak fluent Catalan and 94 per cent understand it. In the Basque Country, 46 per cent speak Basque, but 43 per cent of the people living there cannot understand a word of the language. This language difference is at the heart of difficulties in the Basque Country and a barrier to the closer integration of Basque and non-Basque peoples.

▼ The regional parliament building in Andalucía.

THE BASQUE QUESTION

There is considerable tension in the Basque Country between Basques and non-Basques (mainly Andalucíans from southern Spain, whose forebears moved there during the nineteenth century). The two cultures have never integrated, especially as the migrants and their descendants have never mastered the distinct and very different Basque language. This problem of non-integration has come to the fore in the region's politics. Many Basques call for complete independence from Spain in what has become known as the Basque Separatist Movement. In contrast, the non-Basque population supports the national parties. This means that local Basque parties have never achieved sufficient support or power to realize their ambitions, or even to have their interests represented in the same way as, for example, are Catalonia's. In the late 1960s, Basque separatism took a sinister turn when a terrorist group called ETA (*Euskadi Ta Askatasuna*,

meaning 'Basque Homeland and Liberty') began to use violent means – mainly assassinations and bombings – to try to force independence for the region. Nearly 1,000 people have been killed by ETA, and the group's violence continues periodically to the present day. One of the two main Basque separatist parties, Batasuna, is officially banned because it is suspected of having direct links with ETA. The Basque Country could achieve more autonomy under the existing constitution, but for this to happen it would need political agreement among all parties. As long as the separatists continue to demand independence and be associated with terrorism, it is unlikely that such a consensus will occur.

▼ In the year 2000, tens of thousands of protesters took to the rainy streets of Bilbao to call on Basque ETA separatists to silence their guns. The banner reads, in Basque: 'Peace, ETA no.'

A CHANGE OF DIRECTION

During the March 2004 election campaign, Aznar's PP government was facing criticism for its handling of the Doñana disaster (see page 55), worsening diplomatic relations with Morocco, and the unpopular decision to take Spain into the US-led Iraq war. The PP, however, was expected to be re-elected because Spain had prospered under Aznar's rule. Then, three days before the election, on 11 March 2004, Madrid was hit by a series of commuter train bombings in which 191 people were killed and more than 1,800 were injured. As Spain tried to deal with the aftermath of the atrocity, Aznar's immediate response was to blame ETA for the attacks. Evidence to the contrary was suppressed, despite suspicions (later proven to be correct) that Islamic fundamentalists were behind the bombings. Angry at having been misinformed, the Spanish electorate voted the PP out of office and returned the PSOE to power under a new coalition with Spain's regional socialist parties. One of the first actions of the new prime minister, José Luis Rodriguez Zapatero, was to keep his election pledge and withdraw Spanish troops from Iraq. Since then, his government has focussed on human rights laws, such as equal rights for women and homosexuals, restricting the power of the Church, and reviewing the complex issue of the autonomies and their rights within the constitution.

► In Barcelona, in 2004, citizens placed candles on the pavement in a vigil to condemn the Madrid train bombings.

Focus on: Women in politics

In 2004, the newly elected José Luis Zapatero's cabinet had an exact balance of male and female members, giving women an equal role at the forefront of Spanish political life. Spain's regional political system provides greater opportunities for young and upcoming politicians, and women are as increasingly likely as men to take advantage of such opportunities. Housing Minister María Antonia Trujillo and Development Minister Magdalena Álvarez. are among the key women in Spanish politics.

CHAPTER 6

Energy and Resources

Spain's conventional energy resources are limited. It has only one small offshore oil field in the Mediterranean and some low-grade coal deposits in the Basque Country and Asturias. The vast majority of Spain's energy needs are met through imported resources. Spain's Mediterranean and Atlantic coasts have oil terminals for transferring imported oil, via a network of pipelines, to refineries throughout the country. Another pipeline beneath the Mediterranean carries gas from Libya and Algeria, and liquified natural gas (LNG) is imported by ship. An extensive network of gas pipelines serves most homes and businesses and has replaced the use of bottled butane gas, though this is still used in areas where connection to the gas network is not economically viable.

ELECTRICITY

Spain's electricity needs are met by coal, gas, hydro-electricity (HEP), nuclear power and renewables, such as wind and solar power. There are concerns over the safety of nuclear power, so its use in Spain is controversial. Following the Chernobyl disaster in 1986, in which a nuclear reactor exploded in the Ukraine (formerly part of the USSR), Spain halted the expansion of its nuclear energy industry. In Spain itself, the Vandellós nuclear power station was forced to close following a fire there in 1989. Nevertheless, the status of nuclear power is being reconsidered because of Spain's reliance on oil supplies (which fluctuate in price on the world markets) for generating much of its electricity. Supporters claim that improvements in reactor design meet the safety concerns of critics and point out that, as a low emissions industry, nuclear power would reduce Spain's greenhouse gas emissions. Critics of nuclear power argue instead for lower energy consumption and greater use of renewable forms of energy.

▼ The nuclear power station at Vandellós in Catalonia, which was closed down in 1989.

RENEWABLE ENERGY

In 2007, Spain had the third largest wind power capacity of any nation, beaten only by the USA and Germany the world leader. Spain's mountainous terrain and reliable winds are ideal for wind farms, and the industry has government support. The regional government in Galicia, for example, has set ambitious targets to meet 55 per cent of its electricity demand from wind power by 2010. The development of wind power could meet energy needs and provide considerable employment opportunities. Spain is fast becoming a world leader in the development and manufacture of wind technology.

One problem is that the locations most suited to wind farms are also in some of Spain's most beautiful landscapes. The turbines and cables necessary to distribute the electricity have a considerable visual impact on these landscapes, and some people are wary about the impact of any expansion of wind farms. Other countries have resolved this issue by locating wind farms offshore, but Spanish fishermen are concerned that offshore wind farms in the Mediterranean could disrupt the region's important fishing industry.

For future electricity needs, Spanish planning focuses on locating electricity generating facilities as close as possible to existing infrastructure (cables, pylons, etc.) and centres of consumption (towns, industries, etc.). Such planning helps to minimize environmental impacts and reduce costs and energy losses (energy is lost during transportation along high voltage cables).

▲ In Galicia, wind farms have a visual effect on the environment and are located far away from most consumers.

 Did you know?

Spain has pioneered a unique source of alternative fuel. At a special plant in Palencia, Andalucía, the pulp left over from pressing olives to make olive oil is used as fuel for generating electricity. Elsewhere in Spain, 'combined cycle' plants also use almond husks, wheat stubble and domestic refuse combusted with conventional fuels to generate electricity.

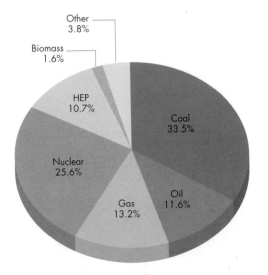

Other 3.8%
Biomass 1.6%
HEP 10.7%
Coal 33.5%
Nuclear 25.6%
Gas 13.2%
Oil 11.6%

▲ Electricity production by type

Wave power (electricity generated by the movement of the sea) is being considered, because generating plants can be located close to ports or coastal settlements with a high demand and an existing infrastructure. To assess the potential usefulness of this technology, the Spanish power company, Iberdrola, has set up a full-scale experimental wave power plant on the Atlantic coast near Santander. However, environmentalists are concerned about the impact that wave technology might have on the rich but fragile habitat for marine life in Spain's northern coastal waters.

Solar power captures the sun's energy as direct heat and light energy, or converts it into electricity using photovoltaic (PV) cells. Although PV cells are relatively expensive, they can provide the cheapest form of electricity in remote locations where the cost and environmental impact of other methods is high. In such circumstances, regional government grants are available to assist with the installation of PV systems. In direct forms, solar energy is used to heat water for domestic or industrial use. But the amount of hot water produced is small and unreliable, so it is usually used domestically to supplement other forms of energy. New buildings in Spain must be designed with energy efficiency in mind, and solar water heaters are therefore a common sight on many homes.

MINERAL POVERTY

Spain has very few mineral resources. Asturias and the Basque Country have poor quality deposits of coal and iron ore that were historically significant in establishing Spain's steel and shipbuilding industries. Today, the raw materials are imported instead. Andalucía has deposits of non-ferrous metals such as zinc (used for galvanizing metals, and in alloys, skin creams, car tyres and cell batteries) and copper (used for heat and conductive properties) that are extracted for domestic use or export.

Energy data

- Energy consumption as % of world total: 1.3%
- Energy consumption by sector (% of total):

Industry:	36
Transportation:	39
Agriculture:	3
Services:	7
Residential:	15

- CO_2 emissions as % of world total: 1.2
- CO_2 emissions per capita in tonnes p.a.: 7.6

Source: World Resources Institute

◀ Combined cycle plants generate electricity using natural gas and alternative fuels, like domestic rubbish. This plant near Tarragona uses by-products from a neighbouring chemical works.

WATER

Spain's most important natural resource is its water, which is vital to the agricultural sector that supplies produce for the European market and beyond. The best agricultural land is in the southern and eastern regions of Andalucía, Murcia, Valencia and Catalonia. These arid regions border the Mediterranean Sea, but lack significant water supplies. The crops grown here include wheat, olives and vines that are less dependent on water. However, if more water were available, then higher value (both economically and nutritionally) fruit and vegetables could be grown.

 Did you know?

The Canary Islands have developed desalination plants to meet their water needs. This technology is now being considered for mainland Spain as an alternative to the PNH.

Focus on: The Plan Nacional Hidrológica (PNH)

In June 2001, the Spanish government announced the PNH, an ambitious scheme to boost water supplies for urban needs and to meet irrigation demand. The PNH would involve building 120 dams, diverting the Ebro River to supply Catalonia, Valencia, Murcia and Andalucía. The PNH drew immediate criticism from local and international environmental groups who were concerned about the Ebro delta. This is an important wetland covering some 320 sq km (123.5 sq miles) and is Spain's second largest ecological reserve.

Environmentalists argued that diverting water from the Ebro River would threaten the delta by allowing the sea to encroach inland, destroying the existing habitat. Amid these concerns, the newly elected prime minister, José Luis Zapatero, ordered a review of the PNH in April 2004 and cancelled the Ebro River transfer, the most controversial part of the plan.

◀ Water being extracted from the Ebro River to irrigate the delta rice plantations. The PNH would have taken water from further upstream.

CHAPTER 7

Economy and Income

Spain is a modern, industrialized nation with a diverse economy, but it is heavily dependent on two sectors – agriculture and tourism. Many other sectors, such as banking, transport, catering, retail, manufacturing and food processing, are reliant on the business generated by agriculture and tourism.

REGIONAL AGRICULTURE

Differences in climate and in the physical geography of Spain mean that agriculture varies from one region to another. Ownership and management of the land also produce regional variations. In southern and central Spain, farming often takes place on large and heavily mechanized estates. Farms still need labourers, however, and these are in short supply in some areas. In northern and eastern Spain, farms are generally smaller family-owned businesses. Some are traditional and have changed little over the years, while others have succeeded in developing markets for specialist produce such as wine and cheese. One problem facing small farms is a lack of resources to develop their businesses. Quality assurance schemes, called *denominaciones*, help to overcome such problems by enabling small producers to combine their resources in areas such as advertising. By this method, produce can be labelled in a way that assures consumers of its quality.

In Spain's mountainous areas, farming requires specific interventions to cope with issues of climate, terrain and remoteness. In some rural areas the farming way of life is maintained by integrating agriculture with compatible activities like small-scale, environmentally sensitive tourism (often known as ecotourism). This provides an additional source of income as farm buildings can be let for accommodation and local produce can be sold to visitors.

Economic data

- Gross National Income (GNI) in US$: 1,321,756,000,000
- World rank by GNI: 8
- GNI per capita in US$: 29,450
- World rank by GNI per capita: 36
- Economic growth: 3.9%

Source: World Bank

▼ These small farms and vineyards in the Priorat region are benefiting from quality assurance schemes.

A CO-OPERATIVE IDEAL

For several generations, Spain's small-scale farmers have worked together in agricultural co-operatives. Among other things, this enables them to afford to invest in large pieces of equipment and larger operations, such as olive presses. During the industrialization of farming, further co-operatives emerged to take advantage of new opportunities in sectors such as food processing and winemaking. Today many farming co-operatives, such as CAG Guissona in Catalonia, resemble industrial corporations. CAG Guissona supplies feeds, veterinary and technical services to farmers and buys their produce, but it also processes, distributes and markets the produce in its own shops and even restaurants. CAG Guissona also offers fuel distribution, banking and insurance services to the general public.

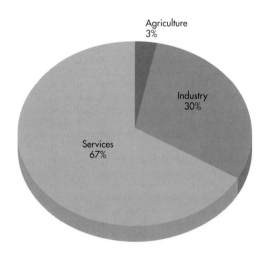

Agriculture 3%

Industry 30%

Services 67%

▲ Contribution by sector to national income

SPAIN AND THE EU

The forerunner of the European Union, the European Steel and Coal Community, was formed by six countries in 1952. Spain joined the EU (then known as the European Economic Community) in 1986. In 2007, the EU expanded to 27 member countries. Spain has benefited enormously from its EU membership. EU development funds have boosted agriculture and helped Spain expand production of high value produce such as olive oil, fruit, vegetables and wine. EU membership has also helped Spain to import foodstuffs (EU members do not have to pay expensive import taxes on internally traded goods) such as meat and dairy produce. Spain's climate and terrain mean that these are difficult to produce domestically.

▲ The modernization of agriculture is important to the Spanish economy, as the potential is enormous. Here rice is stored in perfect condition in huge grain silos on the Ebro delta.

Until Spain joined the EU, import controls protected its manufacturing from international competition. This resulted in inefficiency and poor management. During the 1960s, an abundance of cheap labour made Spain attractive to foreign investors wanting to produce goods in Europe. Foreign investment, particularly in the automobile and petrochemical sectors, helped to improve efficiency in Spanish industry. For example, the SEAT car firm was set up under Franco and was typical of the old, inefficient Spanish industries. In 1990 the German car company Volkswagen bought SEAT and greatly improved its efficiency.

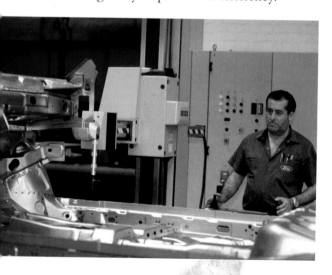

▲ A worker at a Ford car plant in Spain operates machinery on a production line for the 'Ka' vehicle. The finished cars will be sold throughout Europe.

The EU expansion from 15 to 27 members has threatened further foreign investment. Many of the new EU members are former Soviet bloc countries. Production costs are lower in these countries and they have better access than does Spain to the main European markets. Several multinational companies, such as Phillips and Samsung, have already relocated to these Eastern European countries.

INDUSTRIAL DECLINE

Several Spanish industries face external competition as well as competition within the EU. For example, Spain's textile industry (important in Catalonia and Valencia) faces competition from Latin America and Asia, where labour costs are cheaper. Mining, steel production and shipbuilding, once a mainstay of the economy in Asturias, Galicia and the Basque Country, have been declining for decades as a result of bad management, poor investment and dwindling natural resources. The nationalized shipbuilder IZAR receives government grants to continue operations, but similar heavy industries have virtually disappeared in the face of cheaper overseas competition. As a result, these areas now suffer economic problems such as low incomes and high unemployment. Despite losses in their mineral and textile industries, Catalonia and Valencia have fared better. Their mercantile traditions and the greater availability of private capital have helped to develop enterprises in engineering and consumer goods. The tourism industry in these regions also helps them to survive setbacks in other sectors. The regional governments (*Generalitats*) have made considerable investment into infrastructure

 Did you know?

Spain's construction industry is the biggest growth sector in the economy. Huge projects like airports, railways and water management schemes have boosted the economy and led to increased demand for housing and factories. There is concern, however, that house price inflation combined with high domestic debt, a saturated market and possible increases in interest rates could threaten its continued growth in the future.

(transport and communications networks), and education and research facilities. This has created a well-educated workforce with a good standard of living that has, in turn, attracted high-technology industries from around the world, such as Dow Chemicals from the USA and SmithKline Beecham from the UK, to locate to these regions. More than 3,000 foreign companies now operate in Catalonia.

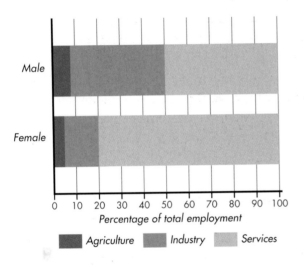

▲ Labour force by sector and gender

Percentage of total employment

■ Agriculture ■ Industry ■ Services

▲ EU development grants support vital infrastructure improvements, for example, the building of bridges and roads. Spain's road network is opening up to previously isolated areas, such as Asturias.

Focus on: Tourism

In 2006, tourism accounted for 5 per cent of Spanish GNP. Mass tourism to Spain started in the 1960s and this industry has been of great economic benefit. There has recently been an increase in specialist markets, such as 'city breaks' and 'ecotourism', but mass tourism and the 'package holiday' remain dominant. In 2006, Spain received 58.5 million international tourists, second only to France. Spain surpassed France in international tourism earnings, with US$57.5 billion (only the USA earned more in tourism revenue). The introduction of the Euro currency in January 2002 has made it easier for tourists to compare the costs of holidaying within the Eurozone (the twelve countries that adopted the Euro currency). Competition between destinations has therefore increased, and jobs in tourism tend to pay poorly as a result. Employment in tourism is highly seasonal, a factor that creates periodic labour shortages (when jobs are often filled by immigrants), and high social security spending for the government as unemployment soars in the off-season.

CHAPTER 8

Global Connections

Spain's era of empire ended in the nineteenth century as it lost its colonies and Spanish leaders began to adopt a policy of isolationism. In the twentieth century, Spain's isolation from international affairs continued because much of the outside world was reluctant to do business with the Franco dictatorship. In the 1950s, however, Spain was suffering economic hardship and needed help. Franco therefore allowed the USA to build military bases in Spain in return for aid (in the form of rent). Franco's regime appeared to grow less authoritarian and, in 1955, Spain joined the United Nations (UN); membership of other organizations was not permitted, however, until after Franco's death. In 1982, Spain joined the North Atlantic Treaty Organization (NATO) that had been established following the Second World War. Spanish troops have since taken part in NATO operations in Kosovo and elsewhere. Changes in Spain's legal and financial institutions paved the way to the country joining the EU in 1986.

COMPLEX RELATIONSHIPS

In 2003, US-led military action in Iraq exposed the complexity of Spain's international relations. Spain's support for the USA was deeply unpopular with the majority of Spaniards, many of whom believed the US military presence in Spain during the 1950s was in support of Franco. The US military presence in Spain remains a controversial issue today. In March 2004, the Madrid bombings (see page 25) were believed to be a direct result of Spain's involvement in Iraq. A change of government and the withdrawal of Spanish troops from Iraq quickly followed. Other European nations, including France and Germany, were always opposed to US action in Iraq and Spain's involvement has left it in a difficult position. Today's government is torn between diplomatic loyalties to the EU on the one hand, and to other global allies such as the USA on the other.

COLONIAL TIES

Spain's relationship with former colonial territories in Latin America benefits from a common language (Spanish) and shared cultural values. The importance with which Spain regards its links with Latin America is reflected in overseas investment (in recent years Spain has used EU funding for this purpose). Such investment is considered necessary because many 'Spanish' enterprises are actually

▲ Container ships at Barcelona port, one of the busiest in the Mediterranean area.

foreign owned. This means that decisions made elsewhere could negatively affect the Spanish economy. Investing in Latin America acts as a counterbalance to this risk. In the services sector, banks like BBVA and utility companies like Telefónica have become well established in Latin America. Repsol-YPF is a leading petroleum producer there, supplying local markets and Spain. Foreign investment is always risky, however, and BBVA suffered heavy losses during an Argentinean financial crisis in 2002. Despite the common language, and legal and business frameworks, other problems have also been encountered. Telefónica has found it difficult to set the tariffs it would like and was forced by Peruvian President Alejandro Toledo to reduce its charges. Firms like Repsol-YPF have also been criticized for failing to train local people and for keeping senior management within Spain.

▲ Spanish-owned banks are well-established in Latin America. This photo shows a branch of the BBVA bank in Mexico City.

Did you know?

On average, there is a new docking of a US warship somewhere in Spain every day, and there are more than 8,000 US military flights through Spanish airspace annually.

Did you know?

The Spanish armed forces provide specialist rescue teams to help in disasters such as the tsunami in South-east Asia in 2004 and the earthquake in Kashmir in 2005.

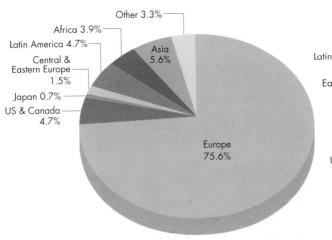

▲ Destination of exports by major trading region

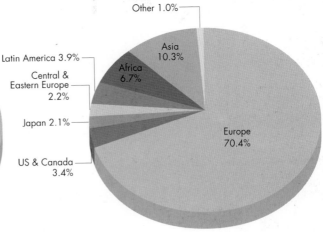

▲ Origin of imports by major trading region

INTERNATIONAL DIPLOMACY AND CULTURE

In 2005, the newly elected Spanish Prime Minister Zapatero conducted a tour of Latin America to strengthen diplomatic relations. These had become strained in the past because of differences in political outlook: many Latin American countries have had a succession of military leaders and dictatorships. As these countries pursue more democratic policies, Spain has recognized the importance of forging closer international relations. Cultural links are already strong and growing stronger, as expatriate communities from countries like Ecuador, Colombia, Argentina and Chile increase in Spain. Besides, Spain has provided employment for immigrant workers and given refuge to people fleeing periods of political instability in Latin America. As the former colonial power, Spain acts in some measure as a keeper of the cultural heritage of Hispanic people everywhere. Government supported cultural organizations like the Cervantes Institute, which offers Spanish language courses and sponsors Spanish literature and theatre, aim to promote 'Spanishness' around the world.

RELATIONS WITH AFRICA

Spain's proximity to Morocco in North Africa means that its relationship with this country is especially important. Spanish-Moroccan ties are influenced by colonial history and by Morocco's claim to Ceuta and Melilla. The dispute over these Spanish enclaves (the only remaining European presence in Africa) reached a crisis in 2002, when twelve members of the Moroccan police landed on the tiny, uninhabited Perejil Island near Ceuta, with a view to taking it over. Spain used disproportionate force to reoccupy the island. Diplomatic pressure was brought to bear by the USA and the EU to avoid an escalation of the crisis. Spain and Morocco also have tense relations over the issue of illegal immigration. Morocco faces a humanitarian problem as tens of thousands of immigrants from sub-Saharan Africa enter the country

◀ Spanish prime minister José Luis Rodriguez Zapatero (right) holds a press conference with the Venezuelan President Hugo Chavez (left) in Madrid during a three-day visit by Chavez to Spain.

illegally, smuggled by international criminal gangs. Under pressure from other EU countries concerned about population growth, the security services of Spain and Morocco are working together to try to prevent illegal immigration.

Spain's other links with African countries include access to fishing grounds off Mauritania and the supply of natural gas from Algeria and Libya. Spain is also involved in attempts to broker peace in the Middle East. In 1991, it hosted the Madrid summit, an important stage in the ongoing peace process between Israel and the Palestinian Authority and a major diplomatic achievement.

INTERNATIONAL AID

Spain is an important international aid donor. It aims to give 0.5 per cent of its GNP annually, and provides technical support, such as paramedical teams, to disaster areas. Spain's regional governments provide a significant proportion of its aid, which is used to support local organizations abroad.

▶ In 2005, a member of the Spanish civil guard talks to would-be African immigrants in Tarifa, southern Spain. The immigrants were intercepted in the Straits of Gibraltar as they attempted to reach Spain in fragile boats.

Focus on: The Rock of Gibraltar

Gibraltar is a UK controlled rocky headland that juts out into the Straits of Gibraltar between Spain and Morocco and at the meeting point of the Mediterranean Sea and Atlantic Ocean. Gibraltar's location means that its occupants can control shipping through the Straits. As a result, its town and port are important to the neighbouring area and particularly to Spain. Many Spaniards commute daily to Gibraltar for work. Spain has long sought to regain sovereignty over Gibraltar, which was signed over to Britain at the Treaty of Utrecht in 1713. However, in local referenda, Gibraltar's people have voted to remain part of the UK. The UK Navy's use of Gibraltar as a strategic base, particularly for the siting of nuclear submarines, causes occasional tensions with Spain. But Spain also benefits from the UK presence because the Navy works closely with Spanish border police to combat illegal drugs and people trafficking across the Straits.

CHAPTER 9

Transport and Communications

Spain's road and rail network radiates outwards from Madrid. Major roads are called *autovias* and *autopistas* (toll roads). The Pyrenees are a major obstacle to the road network and cause bottlenecks because the *autopistas* can only pass through them at certain points at the coastal extremities. Spain exports much of its food produce via road, and the French border at La Jonquera in the Pyrenees is the most direct route to European markets. Congestion here is a major problem, and is made worse in the summer when tourists add to the commercial traffic.

AIR TRAVEL

Spain's national airline is Iberia, and the main international airport is located at Madrid. Barcelona also has an important airport and this, with Madrid, acts as a 'hub' for national air services. The increase in European budget airlines has made regional airports much busier in recent years, especially in tourist areas such as Alicante, Girona or Palma de Mallorca in the Mediterranean.

RAILWAY SYSTEMS

Spain's national rail network is operated by RENFE (*Red Nacional de los Ferrocarriles Españoles*) whose trains run on 'Iberian' gauge (this means the distance between the rails is 1.67 m). In northern Spain and some urban areas, regional governments run additional rail services on different gauges, including 'standard' (1.43 m between rails) and 'metre' gauge (1.00 m). Iberian gauge is particular to Spain and Portugal, which means that RENFE trains cannot run on other systems or cross the French border. Spain opened its high-speed rail network linking Madrid and Barcelona in February 2008. The trains are expected to carry people between the nation's two major cities, at speeds of up to 300 km/h (186 mps).

 Did you know?

A Spanish company, TALGO, has invented specialized trains that are able to switch between standard to Iberian gauge, the main two types of rail track found in Spain.

◀ Aircraft of the national air carrier, Iberia, on the tarmac at Madrid airport. New low-cost carriers across Europe have brought about a rapid increase in air traffic in Spain.

The high-speed link is part of a government promotion of railways for which some 41 billion Euros (US$ 48.4 billion) have been allocated for the construction of rail infrastructure up to 2007. In total, 7,200 km (4,500 miles) of railway, with trains reaching speeds of 350 km/h (220 mph), are planned or under construction. This will bring all of Spain's major cities within four hours travelling time of Madrid, and six-and-a-half hours travelling time of Barcelona.

THE BENEFITS OF RAIL

Rail travel is more energy efficient and less polluting than road transport and often faster. (Same-day goods trains between Madrid and Barcelona are faster and cheaper than road transport.) Railways connecting ports and major industries are also ideal for carrying bulky goods such as coal or cars. Road transport is often still required for the final delivery of goods, but containerization and hi-tech information systems make the movement of goods between rail and road networks very efficient.

Focus on: Air or rail?

Spain's intercity trains face competition from increasingly low-cost air travel and cannot compete with aircraft for speed. However, if the total journey is considered, rail has several benefits. Unlike airports, most train stations are in city centres, so less time is needed at the start and end of a journey. Rail services also have reduced check-in times because passengers accompany their luggage. The biggest advantage is comfort: Spain's modern trains are luxurious, quiet and spacious. Business passengers can continue to work and even use the Internet while they travel.

Transport & communications data

- Total roads: 681,224 km/423,293 miles
- Total paved roads: 681,224 km/ 423,293 miles
- Total unpaved roads: 0 km/0 miles
- Total railways: 14,974 km/9,304 miles
- Airports: 154
- Cars per 1,000 people: 573
- Mobile phones per 1,000 people: 1142
- Personal computers per 1,000 people: 280
- Internet users per 1,000 people: 460

Source: World Bank and CIA World Factbook

▶ Roads and railways used to be built following the lie of the land, but the new high-speed train line (on concrete stilts above the road) goes straight from point to point.

Spain has introduced various schemes to influence attitudes to rail travel and public transport. In most large cities, for example, Barcelona, Bilbao, Madrid, Valencia and Seville, a single ticket allows easy transfer from national rail services to local buses, suburban trains, trams and metro systems. Despite these changes, too many Spaniards still use private motor vehicles to go to work. Between 1990 and 2005, there was an increase in the number of vehicles per 1,000 people by nearly 60 per cent, from 360 to 573.

TELECOMMUNICATIONS

Historically, Telefónica has dominated the Spanish telecommunications industry, operating fixed line services and developing the mobile network. But following liberalization of the industry in 1997, others companies (including Amena, Auna and Vodafone) began to offer competing services. Spain's mountainous terrain and dispersed population makes landline

network coverage problematic, but cellular technology, which has no need for a fixed infrastructure, allows even remote communities to have phone services. As a result of these developments, telephone access in Spain has increased ten-fold since 1975.

In 2008, around 46 per cent of Spaniards were Internet users. A national fibre optic network managed by Telefónica delivers broadband services to most people, using satellite technology to reach remote areas. In addition, Spain's autonomous regions and local government bodies subsidize free public Internet access points.

THE MEDIA

The broadcast media in Spain is divided between public and private ownership. The national service, RTVE, provides two television channels, TV1 and TV2, and *Radio Nacional de España*, which operates local and national news channels and popular and classical music stations. RTVE has a reputation for high quality programming in dramas and documentaries, but state control during the Franco regime means that people are suspicious

▼ Barcelona's new tram (right) provides clean and easy public transport locally, while the luxury intercity coach (left) offers quick and cheap long distance travel.

of RTVE's news coverage. During the news coverage of the Madrid bombings in March 2004, TV1 and 2 maintained the government cover up, despite private news channels broadcasting evidence as it emerged. Private television companies (such as *Antena 3, Canal Plus* and *Telecinco*) operate at the national and regional levels and have a reputation for independent news coverage.

Newspaper readership appears low in Spain at about half the US level and a third of that in the UK. However Spain has no tabloid press, so compared with the readership of the non-tabloid press in the UK or the USA, Spain's readership is similar. Of the national newspapers, *El Pais* and *El Mundo* have a reputation for independence, whereas *ABC* and *El Razon*, show support for the conservative PP party. Besides newspapers, Spain has many popular sports papers, and society news and gossip are covered by the Spanish magazine *¡Hola!*, whose English version *Hello!* and other imitators are printed around the world.

▲ Executives of Spain's largest non-government TV channel, *Telecinco*, pose for a press photo after their company goes public at Madrid's stock exchange on 24 June 2004.

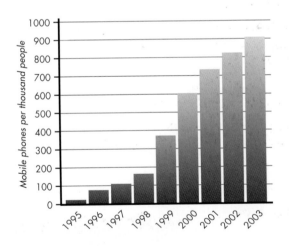

▲ Mobile phone use, 1995-2003

Focus on: ONCE – a national institution

Founded in 1938, ONCE began by providing employment for the blind in running a national lottery. It has expanded to provide social services and specialized education for people with a range of disabilities. It also supports sheltered work schemes, 'special' sports events and campaigns for disabled rights. In 1990, ONCE bought a stake in the *Telecinco* TV station to host its grand lottery draws and promote its activities. Its head, Miguel Durán, became the world's first blind chief executive.

CHAPTER 10

Education and Health

Spain's state education system is based on free and compulsory schooling for children between the ages of three and sixteen. Although free, school places are limited by catchment (where a child lives) and standards vary, so many parents pay for private schooling as an alternative. There are also private day schools (*guardias*) for infants from two years old and, for students over the age of sixteen, there are numerous colleges and universities.

THE SCHOOL CYCLE

Children between the ages of six and eleven undertake *educación primaria* (primary education) and sit yearly examinations. At the age of twelve, children move on to *instituto* (secondary school) and study towards their general leaving certificate, the *Enseñanza Secundaria Obligatoria* (ESO), taken at sixteen. (The ESO is the equivalent of GCSEs in the UK.) Some students continue their studies at *instituto* and take advanced level *Bachillerato Unificado Polivalente* (BUP) exams at eighteen. If they pass their BUP exams, they may take one of two levels of university degree: the *diplomatura*, which is gained after three years' study, and the *licenciatura*, gained after four years.

Higher education is subsidized by the state and students can apply to any university, but most will attend their local one unless seeking a specific course elsewhere. In addition to state-funded universities, there are privately funded universities, including some financed by the Catholic Church. Most university courses are vocational and lead to professional qualifications. The remaining courses are in 'liberal' studies, for example, literature, art, history, etc. Specialized *collegios* control the qualification for certain professions, such as those in medicine and law. They also maintain professional registers and regulate standards of practice.

EDUCATION FOR LIFE

Formación Profesional (FP) certificates are for non-college/university students seeking qualifications for non-professional and technical jobs and work in the public sector. Many private colleges provide FP teaching, and a national *oposiciones* system manages professions in the public sector and allocates jobs to people with FP certificates. However, many Spaniards are dissatisfied with the FP system because people may find themselves with qualifications for which there are no jobs.

▲ Students sit outside Seville University in Andalucia. The university buildings date from 1750.

FOREIGN LANGUAGES

Study of a foreign language in secondary school is compulsory and competence in another language is obligatory for university entry. Traditionally French used to be the second language generally studied, but now English dominates. Other languages are generally studied as options in addition to English. A large number of private language schools have emerged to compensate for a shortfall in English teachers in state schools. However, this lack of teachers is now being remedied, and there are plans to extend the provision of so-called 'immersion' teaching in which general subjects are taught in a foreign language, usually English. Studying English abroad is also very popular with young people, and many students take up European exchange programmes like ERASMUS. For Spanish children, leaving home to study is not generally a traumatic experience because many of them attend summer camps away from home from as young as the age of seven.

Focus on: Regional languages

In the Basque Country, Catalonia and Galicia, students are usually taught in the regional language. In families where Spanish is spoken at home, students easily become bilingual. However, if only regional languages are spoken at school and at home, children may have difficulties writing Spanish correctly. Galician and Catalan are easy languages to learn because they are closely related to Spanish, French, Portuguese and Italian. But Basque is unique and few non-native speakers manage to master the language. Catalan is also spoken in Valencia and the Balearic Islands and in parts of France and Italy. In all, some 11 million people speak Catalan.

Education and health

- Life expectancy at birth male: 76.6
- Life expectancy at birth female: 83.5
- Infant mortality rate per 1,000: 4
- Under five mortality rate per 1,000: 4
- Physicians per 1,000 people: 3.3
- Health expenditure as % of GDP: 8.1%
- Education expenditure as % of GDP: 4.1%
- Primary net enrolment: 99%
- Pupil-teacher ratio, primary: 14
- Adult literacy as % age 15+: 97.9

Source: United Nations Agencies, CIA and World Bank

 Did you know?

More than 30 per cent of primary and secondary school education in Spain takes place in private schools and academies, but private universities award only 8 per cent of degrees.

▼ At Jeréz in Andalucía, children are taught the steps of the flamenco almost as soon as they start school.

service also faces criticism for long treatment waiting times. Together, these factors have led many Spaniards to use private healthcare, which is usually provided by non-profit making assurance societies called *mutuas*. These offer their own services and meet the cost of private hospital bills. People can become members of a *mutua* by paying a fixed monthly fee, which is sometimes met by employers. The private health sector works alongside the state system by contract to the regional health authorities, using its own hospitals to help reduce state waiting lists, or even providing complete services to, for example, primary care centres.

Alternative medicine, using traditional herbal remedies, has a long tradition in Spain. Eastern healthcare, such as acupuncture is also growing in popularity. Cosmetic medicine is also a growth sector.

 Did you know?

Scientists at Barcelona's leading Centre for International Health have discovered a vaccine for malaria, one of the world's deadliest diseases.

▲ Older people are vulnerable to health and social problems. In Spain, widows are often left to struggle with low incomes and poor housing.

HEALTH SERVICES

Regional government authorities provide public health services in Spain following national guidelines. The level of service varies by region, depending on political and economic priorities concerning funding. Demands on the health service may differ from one location to another. For example, in urban centres the service has to cope with the demands of a growing population, while in rural areas it has to meet the expense of reaching isolated communities. General healthcare in Spain is free, but does not include specialist medical branches such as dentistry and podiatry (care of the feet). The

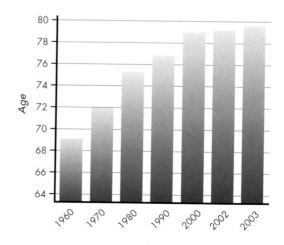

▲ Life expectancy at birth, 1960-2003

NEW HEALTH TRENDS

Spanish people have one of the longest life expectancies in the world. This is often attributed to their Mediterranean diet, based on bread, pulses, fruit, olive oil, and the widespread consumption of fish in preference to a lot of meat or dairy produce. But many older people are afflicted by illnesses linked to malnutrition suffered during their youth, including bone deformities resulting from lack of calcium (derived from milk and other dairy produce).

Recently, overeating has been recognized as another form of malnutrition, and Spanish children rank third in the EU for obesity. The reason for this, partly, is lack of exercise among young Spaniards, the increased presence of meat and dairy products in their diets, and the popularity of fast foods. Obesity-related illnesses such as diabetes are also becoming more common in the adult population.

▶ Spaniards enjoy a wide choice of foods and know the true value of eating well. It is thought that the consumption of fish in preference to meat has greatly contributed to the health of the nation.

Focus on: Health education

Government attempts to provide health education in Spain are hampered by the country's political history and a cultural backlash. For some people, government campaigns are a reminder of the dictatorial control of the media under General Franco. But even when government messages are accepted, a laid-back attitude, which is something of a national characteristic, means that they are often poorly enforced. This is particularly the case with a ban on smoking in public areas, for example. Although many adults have given up smoking, the continued use of tobacco, especially by women and young people, is a worrying trend.

CHAPTER 11

Culture and Religion

Spain enjoys a wide range of popular culture such as pop music, jazz and film. It also has a rich artistic heritage. Spain's most famous painting, 'Las Meninas' by Diego Rodríguez de Silva y Velásquez (1599-1660), hangs in Madrid's El Prado, one of the world's most prestigious art galleries. Pablo Picasso (1881-1973) is perhaps Spain's most famous artist, an Andalucían who spent his formative years in Barcelona at the height of the Modernist movement (1895-1904). Modernism, or *Noucentisme* as it was called, is Spain's unique contribution to international architecture.

Building on a rich heritage of Arabic and gothic architecture, the awesome buildings of modernist architect Antoni Gaudí (1852-1926) attract visitors from all over the world to wonder at the brilliant Catalan craftsmanship.

RELIGIOUS BELIEFS

Spain is an overwhelmingly Catholic country, but relatively few people are regular churchgoers. Catholicism was enforced in Spain following the expulsion of Muslims and Jews in 1492 and the Church was often used as an arm of the state (for example, during the Spanish Inquisition of 1480 to 1835). Such powers continued to be exercised during Franco's dictatorship, when church committees censored all aspects of culture, including films, literature and the theatre. Today, however, the Church and state are clearly separated, but the Church remains a powerful organization that maintains an important aspect of the national cultural heritage and provides a focus for charity work. Religious tolerance is now the norm in Spain, and other Christian denominations and world religions such as Islam are well represented. Across Spain, new places of worship have been built to house these congregations. There has been some local opposition to the building of new mosques because residents are concerned that they might draw yet more immigrants to their *barrio*.

◀ Architect Antoni Gaudí died when work had just begun on the Sagrada Familia church in Barcelona. Gaudi designed this and other extraordinary buildings in Barcelona, creating one of the most exciting cityscapes in the world.

FESTIVALS AND PILGRIMAGES

Spain's most important religious festival is
Easter, marked by solemn parades re-enacting
the Stations of the Cross (Christ's journey to his
crucifixion). Christmas is less significant, but
Epiphany is traditionally celebrated through the
giving of gifts to children in memory of the
three wise men who, Christians believe, visited
Jesus in the manger.

Spain's most important religious site is Santiago
de Compostela in Galicia. In the ninth century,
shepherds claimed they had discovered the lost
grave of St James (one of Christ's twelve
apostles) here. Relics were later found and, by
the eleventh century, Santiago de Compostela
had become a major pilgrimage site, ranking
alongside Jerusalem and Rome. Every year,
thousands of pilgrims still follow the Way of St
James on foot, crossing the Pyrenees at
Roncevalles and visiting numerous famous
shrines along the route. Other religious sites in
Spain include the monastery at Montserrat, the
Catalan national religious centre, and the shrine
of St Rocio near Seville, where one of the most
colourful festivals, or *fiestas*, in Spain takes place.

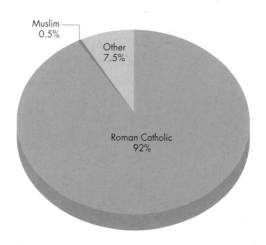

▲ Major religions

 Did you know?

Aimery Picaud, a French monk, wrote the world's
first travel guide about The Way of St James. His
Liber Sancti Jacobi was published in 1130.

▼ Pilgrims cross the Quema River on their journey to
one of Spain's holy shrines in May 2005. Every year,
hundred of thousands of people converge on the
village of Almonte in Andalucía to pay homage to
the Virgin del Rocio.

¡FIESTA!

Spanish *fiestas* are based on some act of religious observance (such as a pilgrimage), celebrating a miracle or a saint's day. Over the centuries, *fiestas* have become more elaborate and can now last for days or even weeks. They form an integral part of Spanish cultural life, and are one of Spain's defining features, whatever the region. The Spanish people's enthusiasm for *fiestas* has never dwindled. *Fiestas* draw together small groups, such as members of a *barrio* residents' association or a company social club, who meet to organize the events and provide the entertainment on the day. Each *fiesta* has its own peculiarities, leading to international renown in some instances. In Alcoy, spectacularly dressed 'Moors and Christians' celebrate the *reconquista* with glittering parades. In Seville, the April fair is an endless display of flamenco music and dancing. Barcelona's *Mercé fiesta* has human castles and the city's squares fill with people performing Catalonia's national dance, the *Sardana*.

▼ At the San Fermin *fiesta* in Pamplona in July 2005, bulls and steers run through the centre of the town to the bullring every morning for the week of the festival.

Did you know?

The arched vaults at Ellis Island in New York were built by Catalan architects. When the hundred-year-old building was restored between 1983 and 1990, only seventeen of its 29,000 tiles were found to be broken.

Did you know?

With his famous work, *Don Quixote*, Miguel de Cervantes (1547-1616) is credited with having invented the novel as a literary form and he is ranked alongside Shakespeare in the history of literature.

Perhaps the most spectacular of all Spanish *fiestas* is San Fermin, in Pamplona, during which young men and women test their bravery by running before herds of savage bulls (known as the 'running of the bulls'). The participants have only a rolled up newspaper each to protect themselves from the bulls' lethal horns! In the Basque Country, traditional games like wood-chopping, stone-hurling and caber tossing are part of *fiestas* and, as in Galicia, sword-dancing and bagpipe music prevail. Even the tiniest villages celebrate *fiestas* with local people dancing the night away. In some famous villages people take part in running street 'battles' using trailer loads of tomatoes or tankers of wine for ammunition. Everyone is invited to join in the fun!

FAMILY FEAST

Besides their religious affiliations, *fiestas* are an occasion for reuniting the family, most often around the kitchen table. Spaniards care deeply about food and are proud of their regional specialities, such as *pulpo Gallego* (octopus Galician style), Catalan *oca amb peres* (goose cooked with fresh pears), *kokotxas á la San Sebastian* (hake cooked with garlic), and *gazpacho Andaluz* (a chilled soup eaten in high summer). The rice, vegetable, poultry and fish dish, *paella*, is wrongly considered by many non-Spaniards to be Spain's most typical dish. Correctly named *Paella Valenciana*, it is in fact a local speciality that *Valencianos* claim should only be made with ingredients from their own region. Some even say that it should only be cooked in Valencian water! Spain's 'national' dish, the *tortilla española*, is a thick pancake of egg and potatoes.

▲ A store in Barcelona selling many types of local ham, sausages and other meats.

Focus on: Blood in the sand!

La Corrida, or bullfighting as it is inaccurately called in English, is a formal dance that is reviewed in the arts pages of the Spanish press, like a ballet or an opera. Despite its artistry, it is a bloody and brutal spectacle, as the bull is systematically weakened by the lances of the *toreadors* and *picadors*, then killed with a single deadly sword thrust by the *matador* (meaning literally the 'killer'). Many Spaniards oppose *La Corrida* for its cruelty and it is banned in many areas. But its supporters are passionate in their defence of what they consider to be an important art form, symbolizing much of what it means to be Spanish.

CHAPTER 12

Leisure and Tourism

Cultural pursuits are an important leisure activity in Spain, benefiting from its rich artistic and architectural heritage. Historic buildings, museums and galleries are popular places to visit, and the performing arts are actively supported. After a long period of decline, brought about by the effect of television which has kept people entertained in their homes, there has recently been a resurgence of interest in music and the theatre. Culture and the arts receive considerable support from savings banks (known as *Cajas*), which are obliged to donate a proportion of their profits to social and cultural patronage. The largest savings bank, *La Caixa*, donated 184 million Euros in 2003.

SPORT

Invented in the Basque Country, *pelota* could be described as Spain's national game. It is similar to the game of squash and is played widely throughout most of the country. *Pelota* is played by two to six players in a walled court called a *cancha*. Players use a curved wicker basket (called a *cesta*) strapped to their hand to hurl a ball against the wall. In addition, most mainstream sports have some representation in Spain, and it is especially well represented in tennis, golf and motor-racing. In 2005, the Asturian racing driver, Fernando Alonzo, became the youngest-ever Formula 1 champion.

TOURISM

Spain has one of the world's largest tourism industries, second only to France in visitor numbers and the USA in tourist earnings. In 2006, tourism accounted for 5 per cent of Spain's GDP.

▲ The 24-year-old Fernando Alonzo in the Shanghai round of the 2005 Formula 1 series in which he became the youngest Grand Prix world champion ever.

However, Spain faces serious competition for tourists from its Mediterranean neighbours and from long-haul destinations like the USA or South-East Asia. In the struggle to attract customers, the Spanish tourism industry has cut costs and this has led to high rates of bankruptcy among local businesses. Spain's heavy reliance on tourism is not always beneficial. Many local businesses do not profit from Spain's tourists because the income goes to mainly foreign-owned tour companies and airlines. Even the government may not gain, because the taxes that tourists pay on their holidays are due in the country where they book their trip and not necessarily in Spain.

The main tourist season is short, from April to October. This means that most tourist workers find themselves laid off for the winter months and sometimes out of work for up to six months each year. Although the government receives revenue from tourist expenditure in Spain, this is offset by the welfare benefits it has to pay to laid-off workers. To make matters worse, the social security contributions of these workers are often low because of the poor pay in the industry.

Local municipalities may also find themselves with substantial costs, as they need to maintain infrastructure and services for visitors who number up to ten times the resident population in peak season. Despite the apparent lack of benefits, the Spanish government supports tourism through government grants and international advertising campaigns promoting Spain as a destination. Tourism generates jobs and creates a demand for goods and produce from other Spanish industries, such as the food and drink industries.

◄ Flamenco music and dance are often used by ballet companies to dramatize classic tales from Spanish literature. In 2004, star dancer and choreographer Sara Baras, seen here, performed the tragedy 'Mariana Pineda' to critical acclaim throughout Spain and abroad.

Focus on: *Futbol* mad!

When it comes to sport, soccer (known as *Futbol* in Spanish) is the true national obsession. Fans are very passionate and fiercely loyal to their teams. They tend to support a local team and the national team, which is one of the best in the world. The biggest *Futbol* event in Spain is undoubtedly the match between FC Barcelona and Real Madrid. These teams contain some of the world's top players and when they meet it seems the entire country comes to a halt. Tickets are sold out months in advance, and roads and towns become deserted on match days as fans gather in bars and cafés to watch the game unfold on television.

▲ Huge resorts like Benidorm on the Costa Blanca provide affordable holidays in the sun for millions of Europeans.

A PLACE IN THE SUN

The Spanish Mediterranean has a climate that is mild all year round. This makes it a popular location for people from across Europe, some of whom have invested in second 'holiday' homes. Many of these visitors plan eventually to retire to their homes in Spain. Although their presence brings a considerable income to Spain, the large proportion of elderly people, many of whom do not speak the languages, can place pressure on local services. The popularity of Spain with senior citizens certainly helps to extend the tourist season, however, and Spanish pensioners who benefit from cheaper 'out of season' holidays are also significant in this respect.

THE SPANISH ON HOLIDAY

Internal tourism accounts for almost half of the tourist sector hotel occupancy in Spain. August is the traditional holiday month for Spanish people, many of whom are seeking to escape the summer heat. The most popular destinations for such tourists are the cooler Atlantic coastlines with their beautiful beaches, elegant resorts and picturesque villages. As incomes rise in Spain, an increasing number of Spaniards are choosing to holiday abroad, so Spain must now compete to keep its own tourists as well as international visitors.

ALTERNATIVE TOURISM

Spain's fastest growing tourist sector is in rural tourism. This benefits from grants and publicity from regional governments aimed to attract visitors to small hotels, farmhouse accommodation, campsites and youth hostels. In mountain areas, where funding is intended to help sustain traditional lifestyles, rural tourism is extremely important. A growing interest in the environment and outdoor pursuits has also led to an influx of tourists to rural areas. Many of these new tourist opportunities brand themselves as 'ecotourism', as they help to sustain rural traditions, generate greater awareness of nature, and have a low environmental impact.

Tourism in Spain

- ▱ Tourist arrivals, millions: 58.451
- ▱ Earnings from tourism in US$: 57,537,000,000
- ▱ Tourism as % foreign earnings: 18
- ▱ Tourist departures, millions: 10.676
- ▱ Expenditure on tourism in US$: 20,348,000,000

Source: World Bank

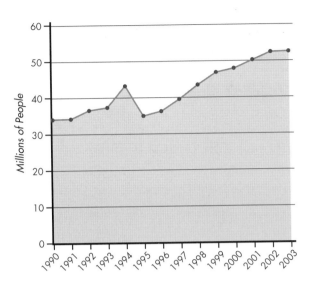

▲ Changes in international tourism, 1990-2003

▲ Disused railway lines make excellent walking and cycle tracks and are suitable for older or disabled hikers. The *Vias Verdes* network of specially adapted lines extends to more than 1,000 kms (620 miles).

Did you know?

The *Grandes Routes* network of walks is being enjoyed by a new generation of young people who have a high awareness of the natural environment. The Pyrenean High Route (HRP) takes more than 45 days through the mountain environment between the Mediterranean and the Atlantic coasts.

Did you know?

The 2005 'Smile, You're in Spain' advertising campaign cost the Spanish government 32 million Euros.

Focus on: The environmental impact of tourism

In 1954, Vladimir Raitz founded Horizon Holidays, which provided tourist flights to Perpignan with a bus connection to campsites along the Costa Brava. Raitz is therefore credited with having invented the package holiday. Although Spain can pride itself on having introduced tourism to a mass market, it has also had to live with some early mistakes. Excessive building development and over-exploitation of natural resources, such as water, have resulted in damaging environmental impact, especially in Spain's most popular destinations, like the Balearic Islands.

In 2002, the regional government of the Balearic Islands introduced a 'green' tax. This was to be levied on tourism and pledged to funds for environmental improvements, but it had to be dropped under pressure from the tourist industry, which had lost 5 per cent of earnings. Coastal nature reserves and stricter environmental laws have helped to reverse the environmental damage along Spain's coasts. But inland areas with more sensitive environments are now coming under pressure from developments such as golf links and ski resorts.

CHAPTER 13

Environment and Conservation

Spain's wilderness areas are an important refuge for animal species, such as bears and wolves, that have disappeared elsewhere in Europe. Spanish habitats are also significant for millions of migratory birds. However, across the country habitats are under increasing pressure from agriculture, urban expansion, infrastructure projects and other human activities.

BRIDGING TWO CONTINENTS

Many birds (particularly larger ones) are unable to travel long distances over water. This means that the 14-km (8.7-mile) Strait of Gibraltar between Spain and Morocco is an essential crossing place for millions of birds migrating between Europe and Africa. The birds need to feed and rest before making the crossing; as a result, Spain has a large and diverse bird population, especially in wetland environments. But the large number of feeding birds also puts great pressure on these sensitive areas. This pressure is intensified by human activities that reduce the habitats available to wildlife.

WETLANDS UNDER THREAT

Wetlands face specific threats from the extraction of river water to meet agricultural and industrial needs. This practice reduces the volume of water reaching the wetlands and results in reduced habitats for wildlife. In addition, wetlands have been drained and built upon, especially in coastal areas with very high population densities. Along the Mediterranean coast, for example, tourism and industrial installations occupy large areas of former wetland. In turn, these have led to the construction of housing for employees and services (such as supermarkets, schools and hospitals) to meet their needs. Wetlands in river estuaries and deltas face particular threats of pollution and disruption from industries, such as petrochemicals and port facilities, both of which are traditionally located near river mouths.

▼ A meadow in the Picos de Europa national park is an example of the beauty of Spain's natural environment.

In 1988, a law called the *Ley de la Costa* was passed with the aim of controlling development in Spanish wetlands. But it has had only limited success, and in many areas the development of wetlands for building continues. For example, on the floodplain of the Francoli River near Tarragona, chemical companies, an oil refinery and a leisure complex all compete for the remaining area of undeveloped land. By contrast, the heavily industrialized Llobregat River in Barcelona has become a successful example of river reclamation in Spain. Its 'greening' project has resulted in part of the estuary being classified as a natural park.

▼ Although it is a natural reserve and vital for migration, the Ebro delta on Spain's north-eastern coast is under constant threat. This luxury housing development is right on the edge of the delta.

Environmental and conservation data

- Forested area as % total land area: 14
- Protected area as % total land area: 8.0
- Number of protected areas: 571

SPECIES DIVERSITY

Category	Known species	Threatened species
Mammals	132	20
Breeding birds	515	20
Reptiles	67	8
Amphibians	32	4
Fish	187	24
Plants	5,050	14

Source: World Resources Institute

Focus on: The Doñana disaster

In April 1998, a reservoir containing toxic mining waste burst its banks and contaminated almost 11,000 hectares of the Doñana wetlands, a UNESCO world heritage site. Poor co-ordination between the regional and national government failed to control the spillage and worsened the catastrophe. Breeding and migratory birds were badly affected by the contamination and long-term effects resulted in many species failing to reproduce. Environmental groups had long warned of such a disaster, but were ignored by the government, which continued to grant mining permits even after the disaster. Environmental groups are now consulted on the management of Doñana, but mining operations and other interests continue to pose a potential threat to its wildlife.

▲ Trees in an orchard near Lleida are treated almost constantly for pests and diseases. This spraying of chemicals kills insects which form part of the food chain.

PROTECTED AREAS

The national parks of Picos de Europa and Ordesa Canyon opened in 1918 as Spain's first protected areas. There are now thirteen national parks in Spain (including the Balearic and Canary islands), covering 326,897 hectares (807,751 acres). Spain also has protected areas classified as natural parks and game reserves. These areas provide vital wildlife refuges but

large predators, like wolves or the Iberian lynx, need huge areas to support the animals upon which they prey. Predators also need to move between territories to maintain their populations, because their offspring search for new territories as they mature. Other animals migrate seasonally in search of food or for breeding.

PEOPLE AND WILDLIFE

Human activity presents many challenges to Spain's wildlife. Roads and railways form barriers to animal movement and agriculture has made large areas inhospitable, clearing them of scrub and using pesticides that destroy any sources of food. Even in Spain's 'empty' spaces, animals soon come into contact with human activity, as in the case of the wild boar.

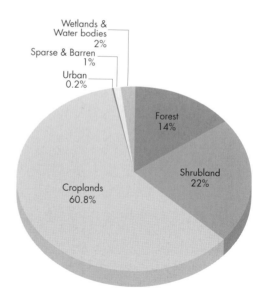

Wetlands &
Water bodies
2%

Sparse & Barren
1%

Urban
0.2%

Forest
14%

Shrubland
22%

Croplands
60.8%

▲ Habitat type as percentage of total area

 Did you know?

One of the world's most spectacular birds, the bearded vulture, has been successfully reintroduced into the Picos de Europa from elsewhere in Spain.

Wild boar can travel up to 25 km (15.5 miles) a day in search of food, and frequently raid crops and fruit trees causing considerable damage. Spanish conservation policy focuses on ways to enable people and wildlife to share their environment. The national parks are a focal point for networks of special nature reserves that limit human activity while protecting livelihoods and culture. The reserves are managed and conserved by the autonomous governments, who also control the development of housing and industry, and the use of land for farming or leisure. Public education about conservation is an important part of Spain's policy and is conducted by training and research centres in the national parks.

HOT PROPERTY

Spain's national parks have successfully preserved some of the most beautiful and unspoilt spaces in Europe, but the use of these and other wilderness areas for human benefit and enjoyment presents major conservation challenges. One such challenge is the risk of forest fire, especially during drought periods that occur every few years in Spain. Fires can be triggered by nature (a lightning strike, for example), but are often caused by human activity, for example, the burning of scrubland (in order to clear it) or the burning of waste in areas near to forests. Overhead electricity cables can also spark fires if trees are allowed to grow too close to them. Since the 1950s, reforestation projects have resulted in the planting of pine trees across large areas of Spain. The pine forests have been popular because of their rapid growth, but sufficient firebreaks have not always been provided. Fires in pine forests are especially dangerous and difficult to control, as pine burns with a heat so intense that trees can explode.

◀ Two Iberian lynx cubs huddle together in their enclosure at a zoo in southern Spain. They are the focus of an emergency breeding plan to prevent the Iberian lynx from becoming the first feline species to become extinct since prehistoric times.

CHAPTER 14

Future Challenges

In the years since General Franco's death, Spain has undergone a rapid transformation to become an important European nation with connections across the world. At times the pace and extent of change has been bewildering and, in many ways, Spain is still coming to terms with its new status. For example, many people believe that Spain's decision to join the US-led war against Iraq in 2003 was the action of a country that thought it was more powerful than it is. By ignoring the fact that many of its EU neighbours opposed going to war, Spain's decision to do so damaged diplomatic relations with countries upon which it depends for its economic status. And the reaction of the Spanish people in the election following the Madrid bombings served to remind Spain that its political stability is still fragile.

THE CHANGING EU

Most Spaniards have a real sense of belonging to Europe and the EU. Membership of the EU has helped Spain to move away from its historical isolation and has led to dramatic economic improvements. Politically, too, the EU has allowed Spain to regain some of the global influence it once held. However, the EU was enlarged in 2004 and 2007, and Spain – once a beneficiary of substantial EU funding – is now expected to act as a donor to the EU.

SUSTAINABLE GROWTH

Spain's rapid economic development has cost its environment dearly, as witnessed in the Doñana disaster (see page 55) and the controversial national hydrological plan (see page 29). But there are many positive examples of

◀ Spain is working to balance rapid industrial development with the needs of the environment. The AVE network has been criticized for damaging sensitive habitat. Even if development is confined to specific zones, roads and railways still form a barrier to land animal migration.

▲ In Barcelona, the flags of Spain, Catalonia and Barcelona fly over the *Ajuntament* (city hall).

environmental management that fail to make the headlines, such as Spain's leading role in developing renewable energy. Greater awareness of the environment and of global issues like climate change have led to an increased demand for sustainable development that continues Spain's strong growth, but also better protects its natural heritage.

THE BASQUE QUESTION

The violence of the Basque separatist group ETA has never been supported by the majority of Basques who would prefer separatism to be achieved through democratic means. The *Cortes* is the only authority able to make the constitutional changes necessary for Basque autonomy or independence, but it must also guard the interests of those Basques who wish to remain part of Spain. Following co-operation between the Spanish and French authorities, many ETA activists have been arrested, leaving the organization in a weakened but still threatening state.

IMMIGRATION

Historically, Spain has tolerated immigration, but more recently there have been isolated racial incidents over perceived conflicts of interest for things like competition for jobs or housing. Legal immigration, however, is essential to the future maintenance of the economy. The government's recent policy of regularizing immigrants to make them full members of Spanish society reflects this need and is intended to improve race relations. At the same time, Spain is under pressure to maintain tight border controls against illegal immigration and human trafficking. This is particularly important given Spain's geographical position as the gateway to Europe for people fleeing from Africa. Spain's relationship with Africa has been central to its past and will remain so into the future.

Timeline

c.1,000-900 BC Migration of Celtic tribes from northern Europe to the *Meseta* and north-west, where they mingle with original Iberian tribes to form the Celtiberian racial group.

c.800-c.500 BC Greek and Phoenecian trading settlements on east and southern coast respectively.

c.400-c.300 BC Carthaginians from North Africa take over much of southern Spain.

218-19 BC War between Carthage and Rome leads to Roman occupation of the Iberian peninsula.

c.200 BC-c.AD 300 Roman colonization completed with the conquest of Asturias and Cantabria.

c.400-c.600 Fall of the Roman Empire and invasion of the peninsula by barbarian tribes. The Visgoths eventually dominate.

c.700-c.800 Moors defeat the Visigoths at the battle of Guadalete in 711. Christians retreat to uninhabited areas in the Cordillera Cantabrica and the Pyrenees. Small kingdoms emerge and the *reconquista* begins.

c.800-1492 The *reconquista* proceeds with numerous alliances between separate kingdoms which now largely form the autonomous regions. The most important of these is the marriage in 1469 of Ferdinand of Aragón and Isabella of Castile. The Christian advance is aided by feuds between rival dynasties of Moors.

1492 Fall of Granada, the last Moorish kingdom to hold out against the Christian advance. Columbus discovers the Americas. Jews and Muslims are expelled from Spain or forced to convert to Christianity.

1516-1700 Under the Habsburgs Spain enters its 'Golden Age' of colonial expansion and artistic enlightenment. But Habsburg misrule ruins the economy and leads Spain into numerous holy wars.

1700-1814 The War of Spanish Succession (1702-14) ends with the Treaty of Utrecht. The Bourbon Felipe V becomes king. Gibraltar is ceded to the English. Catalonia has its autonomous powers removed.

1814-1902 Spain invaded by Napoleon in the War of Independence (1800-14). The century is dominated by wars, *coups d'etat* and foreign interventions. During the Industrial Revolution, Spain fails to keep up with its European neighbours and remains relatively undeveloped.

1898 Spain loses the Spanish-American War and its last colonies in Cuba and the Philippines.

1902 King Alfonso XIII succeeds to the throne.

1923-31 Dictator General Miguel Primo de Rivera governs Spain.

1936-39 The Spanish Civil War.

1939-75 General Franco rules as acting head of state. Political dissent is ruthlessly repressed by torture and death.

1955 Spain joins the United Nations.

1961 First terrorist act by ETA.

1969 Franco names Juan Carlos as his successor.

1975 Death of Franco. Juan Carlos becomes king.

1978 A new constitution is passed by referendum. The Basque Country, Catalonia and Galicia are given varying degrees of autonomy over and above those powers devolved to all the regions.

1981 An attempted military *coup* is thwarted largely as a result of personal intervention by King Juan Carlos.

1982 Socialist Felipe González becomes prime minister.

1986 Spain joins EEC; becomes full member of NATO.

1992 Spain's 500th anniversary celebrations of events of 1492. Madrid nominated as Europe's cultural capital. Seville hosts World Expo '92 fair. Olympic Games held in Barcelona. Spain's new image is spread around the world.

1996 The election of right-wing government under José Maria Aznar.

2004 Fall of the Aznar government following the terrorist bombings in Madrid of 11 March. Spain withdraws from US-led war in Iraq.

Glossary

Ajuntamiento A city or town council. This can be a gathering in a simple village hall or, as in Barcelona, a large organization similar to a regional parliament.

Anarchists People who believe that all forms of government should be abolished.

Archipelago A group of islands.

Autonomous Self-governing.

Caber A long, thick wooden pole.

CiU *Convergència i Unió* The Catalan conservative party.

City break A short package holiday to a popular city destination, e.g. Barcelona, Madrid.

Colonize To transform a community or country into a colony.

Colony A group of people who settle in a country distant from their own, but maintain ties with their homeland.

Communism A political system whereby the state controls the wealth and industry of a country on behalf of its people.

Constitutional monarchy A monarchy whose powers are authorized and limited by a constitution.

Containerization The carriage of goods in standardized containers suitable for road, rail and sea travel.

Democratic Upholding democracy, a political system in which the government is elected by the people.

Desalination plant A place at which salt is removed from sea water, so that the water can be used for drinking or irrigation.

Ecosystem A community of organisms interacting with their physical environment.

Enclave A territory belonging to one state that is surrounded by territory belonging to another.

ERASMUS The European Community Action Scheme for the Mobility of University Students.

Expatriate A person who lives in a foreign country.

Eurozone The countries within the twenty-five-state EU which use the Euro as their unit of currency.

Fascism A political movement that favours centralized, dictatorial government and the repression of political opposition. Fascists tend to hold nationalistic, often racist, views and to believe in firm leadership that does not tolerate dissent.

Firebreak A stretch of cleared land between forest areas over which fires cannot cross and spread.

Gauge The distance between the rails of a railway.

GDP Gross Domestic Product, a statistic which measures the wealth produced, distributed and consumed within a given year. It is often used to measure the 'health' of an economy.

Indigenous Originating in a country or region.

IVA *Impuesto sobre Valor Añadido* Spain's VAT (Value Added Tax) system.

Life expectancy The average period that a person at a specified age may expect to live.

Malnutrition Poorly balanced or insufficient nutrition, including overeating, which impairs health.

Metro The Subway (US) or Underground (UK).

NATO The North Atlantic Treaty Organization, an international organization made up of the USA, Canada and most European countries to guard international security.

ONCE *Organización Nacional de Ciegos de España*, the Spanish national organization for the blind.

Phoenicians An ancient people of north-west Syria, who dominated the trade of the world in 1,000 BC and founded colonies throughout the Mediterranean.

PSC *Partido Socialista Catalana* The Catalan socialist party.

PVC Polyvinyl chloride – a synthetic material used for making hosepipes, insulation, shoes etc.

Rainshadow The relatively dry area on the leeward side of high ground (the side facing away from the wind) in the path of rain-bearing winds.

Referenda Votes on particular, single issues rather than for a political party.

Socialism An economic system that favours ownership of the means of production and wealth distribution by the state rather than by individuals.

Spanish Inquisition An institution that defended the Catholic faith in Spain, mainly by persecuting non-believers and Jews, etc., between the fifteenth and nineteenth centuries.

RTVE *Radiotelevisión Española* The Spanish national broadcasting company.

Subspecies A less numerous variant of a species, with distinct characteristics, usually related to geographical isolation of the population.

Tabloid press Newspapers that carry little in-depth news or analysis, so named because of their small size in relation to the larger papers (broadsheets).

TALGO *Tren Articulado Ligero Goicoechea Oriol* A patented, articulated high-speed train.

Terminal (as in oil terminal) Specialized dock facilities for the unloading of petroleum products from very large ships called 'supertankers'.

Transhumance Human seasonal migration following herded animals.

Transhipment The transfer of goods or passengers from one means of transport to another.

UNESCO The United Nations Educational, Scientific and Cultural Organization: an agency of the United Nations that sponsors programmes to promote education, communication, the arts, etc.

Further Information

BOOKS TO READ

The Changing Face Of Spain
Edward Parker
(Wayland, 2005)

Countries of the World: Spain
Neil Champion
(Evans Brothers, 2005)

Nations of the World: Spain
Nathaniel Harris
(Raintree, 2005)

The New Spaniards
John Hooper
(Penguin, 2006)

Spain Live
Isabel Alonso de Sudea and Kit Davies
(OUP, 2004)

USEFUL WEBSITES

www.iht.com/global.html
Free downloadable version of *El Pais* in English
presented by the *International Herald Tribune*.
Documents are locked to non subscribers of
the *IHT*.

www.ine.es/en/welcome_en.html
Spain's National Statistics Office (Instituto
Nacional de Estadisticas Española) page in
English, with online information and
downloadable reports, especially 'Spain
in Figures'.

http://nuevayork.cervantes.es/en/default.shtm/
The Cervantes Institute's English language site
(based in New York), providing up-to-date
cultural information.

www.energias-renovables.com
Environmental non-governmental organization
specializing in all aspects of the environment,
but especially energy, with an archive of news
items in English.

www.la-moncloa.es
Website of the Spanish government, with
English option. Has links to all government
departments' sites and especially to the
autonomous regions, most of which supply
information in English.

www.ciemat.es/portal.do?IDM:69&NM=1
Spain's Centre for Energy, Environmental and
Technological Research. A very detailed site,
giving up-to-the-minute reports on a range of
research projects.

Index

Page numbers in **bold** indicate pictures.

About the authors

Polly Campbell is a geographer and studied at Sussex and London universities. She has carried out field studies in Spain, Guyana and Morocco. Simon Rice took a degree in Experimental Psychology at the University of Sussex and specialized in psycho-linguistics. He later qualified as a teacher. Both authors have travelled extensively in Spain for more than twenty years and have lived there since 1997.